DRAMA FOR JUNIOR HIGH

Drama for Junior High
with selected scenes

Albert and Bertha Johnson

South Brunswick and New York: A. S. Barnes and Company
London: Thomas Yoseloff Ltd

A. S. Barnes and Co., Inc.
Cranbury, New Jersey 08512

Thomas Yoseloff Ltd
108 New Bond Street
London W1Y OQX, England

ISBN 0-498-07587-7
Printed in the United States of America

Contents

DRAMA FOR JUNIOR HIGH

Part I

YOUR THEATRE WORLD

1

This is Drama

Sports and drama are old teammates. They began together in the first democracy over 2000 years ago in ancient Greece. Young champions of the Olympics were also heroes in the plays. Actors were athletes. They had to be. Actors competing in the drama contests in the annual play festivals had to be in top condition physically and mentally. Winning a prize in the theatre was just as exciting as coming out on top in the Olympic games.

Being in a play today is very much like playing on a team in baseball, football, basketball, or tennis. On the team you play to win the game. On the stage you play to win the audience. In order to win, everyone has to work with everyone else. Everybody shares in the victories and the failures, but the excitement comes from working together and from giving your best to your fellow players. The excitement comes, too, from stretching your muscles and stretching your mind and in getting better and better at what you are doing.

"Getting better" is the objective we mean to discuss. Everything in this book is designed to help toward self-improvement. Even dropouts are usually hopeful of improving their situation. Sometimes they succeed. More often they don't. But in this book we are not discussing dropouts. We are concentrating on winners and potential winners.

Every girl who is taking dancing lessons or plays the piano, and every boy who is out for sports, know that it takes practice to be successful. Practice pays off with rich rewards. Everybody who has had a part in a play knows the value of practice, and the satisfaction that comes with playing the part well. Many have discovered the thrill of that kind of satisfaction even before they enter junior high school.

However, the satisfaction that comes from creative drama, or being in a grade-school play, is kid stuff compared to the kind of achievement we will be talking about in this book. Now is the time to reach toward new horizons and stretch a hopeful hand toward the unreachable star. Sometimes we discover that the unreachable star turns out to be reachable after all, and then, like astronauts, we stretch toward another more distant star. While we reach and while we stretch, we must remember that it is in the reaching and the stretching that we grow. Even if we never quite come up to our expectations, we grow better and stronger through the striving.

Drama, like music and sports and other activities, offers an exciting challenge to everyone who takes it seriously. Fortunately drama is a challenge that almost everyone can enjoy because, as the old saying goes, there is a little ham in each of us. "Ham" is often only a slang expression for talent. Everyone is born with a certain amount of acting talent. Small children are acting when they play at their make-believe games. When the little sister pretends she is the Mommy, and the kid brother imitates the funny guy on television, they are acting. For the very young, acting is as natural as breathing. A baby learns to walk by imitating those who have learned to walk. If a baby could not imitate, he would never get out of his crib. The native ability to imitate is a very important part of the acting talent. It is also a very important part of learning and growing up.

It is true that the acting talent is more than an ability to imitate, but imitation is basic to all acting. Another thing that is basic is the ability to pretend. This is also an ability with which we are born. Little sister pretends she is Mom. The kid brother pretends he is a motorcycle cop, and, as he sputters about on his tricycle, he is fairly convincing.

Children engaged in creative dramatics pretend they are all sorts of different people in all sorts of fascinating situations. In this kind of drama, they are creating the roles spontaneously. Words and actions come easily because they are pretending to be the people they are playing. They pretend, and in their pretending they act as if they really were the characters which they are playing. They act as if their make-believe were really true. The better they do this, the more believable they are, both to themselves and to anyone who may be watching. This is a point to remember because we will discuss ways of achieving believability later in the book.

Of course, drama for junior high is on a higher plane than role-playing and creative dramatics. Nevertheless, the improvisation of creative dramatics is basic to all acting, and the best of professional actors often engage in improvisations. The reason we say drama in junior high school is on a higher plane is that, in junior high, you study and present real plays. In an improvisation, you make up your own words, or lines. In a play you say the lines the author of the play has written. In an improvisation you are usually free to create your own character. In a play you have to interpret the character the author has created. These things call for new kinds of skills and this book deals with those skills.

The skills we will be studying apply primarily to drama for the stage. However, the skills for the stage are basic for drama in television and in motion pictures. T.V. and movies do call for some special techniques, but they all spring from the stage of the living theatre, or live theatre, as it is often called. We must remember that live theatre is much, much older than the movies and television. In fact, the theatre is so old and its history so fascinating that we shall spend several pages tracing its development. An understanding and appreciation of our theatre heritage is essential background for everyone in drama and especially for those eager and curious people who want to excel.

Such words as "excel" and "excellence" will appear frequently in the pages of this book because the encouragement of excellence is our goal. We could say "excellence in drama is our goal," but the goal is not limited to drama alone. In fact, it is hoped that excellence in drama will stimulate a desire for excellence in all fields of learning. Actually, it is more of an expectation than a mere hope, because it has been our experience that young people who excel in drama extend their quest for excellence into all their fields of interest. We expect to excel in those things we enjoy, but once we have had a taste of excellence it is surprising how we become interested in excelling in studies that are less enjoyable. Drama is one of those activities in which we need to know a lot about a lot of different things, and the more we know, the more we can bring to everything we do in drama.

An example of this is the Broadway star who was recently cast as a telephone engineer. As he studied the role while the play was in rehearsal, he took a crash course in telephonics and even went out and climbed telephone poles with the repair men in order to school himself for the part. Another example is that of the actress who played the poetess Elizabeth Barrett Browning in *The Barretts of Wimpole Street,* by Rudolf Besier. The actress gave the role depth by taking a course in romantic poetry.

An actor, even a young actor, will go to great lengths

sometimes in order to do well with his acting assignment. This is especially true when he gets a part he has hoped for. Before play try-outs, students often study with great diligence the roles they hope to get. They don't always get the roles they hope for, and seldom are there roles enough to cast everyone who auditions at the try-outs. Unfortunately, this is especially true for girls, because most plays have more male than female roles. However, when a part is landed the conscientious actor will try to learn everything he can that will contribute to the role.

An interesting fact about drama is that it frequently touches on many areas of information. The student of drama usually discovers that he can use much of what he has learned in other subjects. Even more frequently he will find himself wishing he knew more about many things of which he knows nothing or has only a smattering of knowledge. So it is that drama becomes a great incentive to learning. The more an actor learns, the more he discovers there is still much more to learn. The incentive to learn does two things for him. It sends him off to the library or to his other classes and activities in search of information and knowledge, and it spurs him on to learn more about the theatre and its many fascinating arts.

Having a part in a production, either as a member of the cast or of the production crews, is one of the quickest and surest ways of discovering how much there is to learn about drama and the theatre. While it is true that nearly everyone is born with a certain amount of acting talent, it is also true that talent isn't of much value unless it is developed. A girl may have a talent for baton twirling, but the talent won't be worth much to her unless she gets hold of a baton and goes to work. She must develop her talent through practice. Likewise, a boy may have a rare gift for handling a baseball bat, but he learns to bat by batting.

A musician learns to play by playing, a writer learns to

write by writing, and an actor learns to act by acting. However, there is more to it than just the doing. There are drills and exercises involved, and helpful theories and methods to be studied. A student with a talent which he doesn't bother to develop will rarely get off the home plate. Because of a native talent, he may think he is better than he really is. He may even fool others into thinking he is better than he is. Such an illusion can only end in disillusionment unless he develops his talent through study and practice and experience. Unless he discovers the necessity to develop, he will be surpassed by lesser talents with more industry and ambition.

How does one develop his talent? That is precisely what this book is all about. If talent were a thing that needed no development, there would be no need for a book like this. In fact, there would be no need for teachers, coaches, and directors. There would be no need for practice and rehearsals. If talent needed no development, a squad of young geniuses could trounce the rival team with no coaching and no practicing. A cast, assembled on the spur of the moment, could go on stage and give a finished performance with no director and no rehearsals. Such an idea is so preposterous that we will do well to get on with the business at hand, which is to get this study of drama under way.

Drama. Let us begin with that word *drama*. What does it mean? What is drama? Does it mean the same thing to you that it means to your friends and parents? To your friends it may mean something exciting, even glamorous. To your parents it may merely suggest something with which you shouldn't be wasting your time. There are parents who think that drama is a waste of time. There are school administrators who think that, too. Are they wrong or right?

Drama can be a terrible time-waster. So can any other activity that isn't properly managed. In many schools, drama has a bad reputation. In schools where drama is nothing but a kind of extracurricular hi-jinx with virtually no supervision, it deserves a bad reputation. Parents who oppose that kind of drama and administrators who look down their noses at it are justified, or partially justified. They are certainly justified in condemning any activity that does little for the students other than waste their time, but they would be more fully justified if they took a positive approach to the drama problem. Instead of simply condemning drama, it would be better to condemn the slipshod way in which it is handled. Then, having made that condemnation, they would do better to insist on updating the drama program and placing it in the hands of competent leaders. They would do better to rise above any prejudice they may have against drama and attempt to see it for what it is.

What is it? Whatever else it may be, drama is at least two things. It is an art and it is a remarkable learning process. It is these two meanings that we will be stressing in this book, because these are the meanings that thoroughly justify the inclusion of drama in the schools.

As an art, drama is a form of literature and one of the various theatre arts. Putting it simply, a drama is a play and drama as an activity may include the reading, rehearsing, and performing of plays and a study and practice of everything connected with the performing of plays. Or, to put the latter part of that last sentence another way, "a study of theatre arts and participation in play production."

If a drama is a play, what exactly is a play? We might say that a play is a story told in action and dialogue. It is a story which the characters act out. When the play is presented for an audience, it is the actors who act it out as they interpret the characters. The text of a play may be printed in a book and read to himself by one person in silence, and the reader may himself imagine the action and the sound of the dialogue. But, essentially a play is meant to be performed for an audience, and there were plays long before there were books, even long before the invention of the printing press.

Plays are to the subject of drama what musical scores are to a symphony orchestra. Yet there is this difference. Actors may improvise a play complete with characters, dialogue, story, and action. They have done so through the centuries, as we shall see in a later chapter. Musicians can also improvise, and sometimes do so in what they call "jam sessions," but such musical works as symphonies are read from the score by the musicians. Basically, a musician plays from a score and an actor plays from a script.

There are many kinds of plays. There are plays called tragedies, plays called comedies, farces, melodramas, and many other dramatic forms.

If you were asked to describe the difference between a comedy and a tragedy, could you do it? Could you describe a farce or a melodrama? If you could, fine! As for you—! If you couldn't—well, let's go into that in a moment. First, let's go back to that question "What is a play?" We've explained what it is, but we need to know a lot more about the elements of a play before we can discuss the different kinds of plays. What are the elements of a play? In other words, what are the things a play must have in order to make it a play? One way for you to find out is to try writing a play. Impossible? Well, let's try!

So, you're writing a play! What is your play about? In answering that, you state your subject. So we might say that one element of a play is the subject, or we might call it the theme. You will also tell me that your play is about people. What do we call people in a play? Characters. So, your play must have characters. Element number two—your play must have characters.

What about these characters? What do they do? What happens to them? As you answer these questions, you will find that you are telling a story. So now your play has a story. In this story we will probably discover that some of the characters want certain things, certain things that other characters in the play don't want them to have. The result is conflict. The good guys against the bad guys—conflict is now added to the elements.

Now we have theme, story, characters, and conflict. There is conflict in a football game, and that conflict results in something called "action." Add action to your elements. In football we don't know how the game is going to end. That is also usually true of a play. As the author, you know, of course, but the audience, like a crowd at a ballgame, is kept in suspense. Suspense is a close cousin to action. Action is the element that keeps things happening. Suspense is the uncertainty about how things are going to happen and about how the happening will turn out.

Action has to lead to something. If you've studied physics you know that every action results in reaction. The same is true in a play. In a play, action and reaction create a crisis. Crisis! Add that to your list of elements.

In the game, the rival team has the ball on your one-yard line. The score is tied in the last minute of the game. The rival team has two downs to go. Crisis! Your team holds firm on the first try. On the second and final play there's a fumble and your quarterback recovers the ball. Aided by your center and your right guard, he plows through the line and runs the length of the field for a touchdown. Climax! The reaction to crisis is climax. Add that to your play.

In the game, your quarterback is the hero. Does the play have a hero? Who is he? He is the one who is most affected by the action. He, or she (you may have a heroine), is the one that your story is about. He is the one who figuratively carries the ball and gets the good guys out of the jam. In drama, the hero or heroine is the protagonist. Every play must have a protagonist.

The protagonist must have opposition; otherwise, there would be no conflict. In the game, the opposition is the rival team. In the play, the opposition is called the "antagonist." The antagonist is the villain of the piece. So you can now add protagonist and antagonist to your list of elements.

What next? Dialogue! You are writing a play, not a pantomime. Therefore your characters must engage in conversation. That conversation is called "dialogue." Dialogue consists of the lines or the words the characters speak. They could speak all their lines seated comfortably in a circle on the stage. They could do this, and the play would still have conflict and action. Reaction would not be physical but it might be, nonetheless, dramatic. But something is missing. Unless your play is being given a reading performance, something is missing.

That something is spectacle. Spectacle is the visual aspect of the play. As the characters of the play move about the stage and form various groupings, they are presenting the element of spectacle. Spectacle may also include scenery, costumes, light, and properties.

One more question regarding the elements of a play— what does your play say? What is its message? Can you sum up the thrust of the play in a single sentence, or better still, a phrase? Can the gist of the play be expressed in some such phrase as "Love conquers all"; "Honesty has its price"; or "Stupidity gets what stupidity deserves"? If you can, your premise is clear. Premise is the word. Premise is an element of drama. Every play worth producing has a premise. Directors may not always agree that the premise is what the author thinks it is; however, the author should be clear in his own mind regarding the premise.

Theme, story, characters, conflict, action, crisis, climax, dialogue, protagonist, antagonist, spectacle, and premise—these are the elements of drama. When you look at them as a list, they are formidable. However, when you think about each element one at a time, it is easy to see how important they are to any play. When you take them one at a time it is also easy to look at them with confidence. You may not really want to write a play yourself, but knowing the elements of a play makes it easier to understand a play and should make each play you read much more interesting. Knowing the elements will also help you in your acting. You can act with much more intelligence when you know how a play is put together as well as what it says. On the other hand, you may want to write a play. Well, what's stopping you? Not the elements! You know the elements of drama. So, playwright, write your play.

If you write a play, what kind will it be? Will it be a tragedy or a comedy? Will it be a melodrama or a farce? There are many kinds of plays, such as comedy-drama, high comedy, low comedy, sentimental comedy, comedy of manners, etc., etc.—it will be interesting some time for you to explore the various kinds of plays. However, if we should try to cover them all in this book we should not have room for things that seem more important. It is important to know the difference between comedy and tragedy. It is also important to know the difference between farce and melodrama.

That quarterback who made the touchdown in the last minute of the game! Make him the hero of your play, and you have a comedy. At least, you have a comedy from your point of view. However, to the playwright seated in the opposite bleachers, the play has a tragic ending. Perhaps tragic is too strong a word. The ending is not "a happy one." The ending is important. If the hero wins, the play is a comedy. If he loses, the play is a tragedy. If you have the idea that comedy has to be funny, you're wrong. A comedy may be very serious. A tragedy, on the other hand, may be filled with comedy lines and situations. The test is in the ending. If everything turns out all right for the protagonist, the play is a comedy. This does not mean that the play has to have a happy ending. Not necessarily—the play may end on a very sad note, but if we know the protagonist is victorious, then the play must be considered a comedy. If, on the other hand, the protagonist goes down to defeat, if he loses the thing he has been fighting for, if he fails, even if he fails heroically, the play is a tragedy.

In the classical tragedy of the Greeks, there was never any trace of comedy. Nor was there ever any hint of tragedy in the classical comedies. The Greeks were purists. Was that good? That is a question you may enjoy thinking about later in the book. Look for the challenge to this purist idea. The concept of tragedy has changed through the centuries. One change has been in the tragic hero. Traditionally, the tragic hero must be a person of magnitude, a person who is potentially good and great, a person who can move the audience to awe and pity. In tragedy the audience is moved through horror and compassion to a kind of emotional cleansing. In the old tragedies the protagonists were usually kings or queens or gods. In modern tragedy, the common man may be protagonist. However, there must always be something worth saving about a tragic hero, just as there must always be some flaw in his personality that brings about his downfall.

If you think of tragedy as something that is glum and gloomy you should read more tragedies. Better still, you should see more tragedies. When you have seen, or even when you have read more tragedies, you may discover, as millions have through the ages, that they are plays of great beauty and power. If you have an idea that you simply don't like tragedy, you may be selling yourself short.

Donald, a husky football guard, didn't like tragedy

until his older brother brought home a copy of Shakespeare's *Macbeth* from high school. Don started reading the play and couldn't put it down. Now he is a tragedy buff.

Great tragedy, like great music, is character building. It expands the mind and stretches the soul. Give yourself the chance to stretch and expand.

Comedy is closer to you. Nobody will deny that. Tragedy is something you reach toward. Comedy is more within your grasp. Most of the acting you do will be in comedy or in comedy-drama. This is as it should be, but don't think there isn't challenge in comedy. Later in this book you will learn more about that challenge, and, hopefully, discover ways to meet it. Comedy is the sunny side of life, but even the sunny side has shadows. In comedy you move through light and shadow toward a positive end. You grin through gloom and laugh your way through circumstances. Comedy is triumph over circumstances. Comedy may sometimes be hilarity. It is always joy.

If comedy is sometimes hilarity, what is farce? It is always hilarity, or almost always. Farce is a lot of improbable situations presented as though they were possible. In farce the characters are usually exaggerated, but the exaggeration must always seem to be plausible. In farce, situations are usually more important than characters. The situations may be incredible, but they must be incredibly funny. If a farce is not basically funny, it is not really a farce. It may be satirical. It often is. It may be brilliantly witty. It often is. The sharper the wit, the more stinging the satire, the more the play is likely to fit the form of farce.

Do you like to hiss the villain and cheer the hero? If so, you like melodrama. In melodrama the villain is very very bad and the hero is very very good. The heroine is innocent and pure; the hero noble, brave, and strong; and the villain is a cad, a crook, a scoundrel you like to curse. At least, such is the case in the old nineteenth-century melodramas. Those are the plays that are fun to revive, but don't let them give you a false idea of melodrama. Melodrama can be good, and even great. It may surprise you to learn that Shakespeare's *Macbeth* is a melodrama. It is a tragic melodrama.

What, then, is melodrama? It is a play in which the story or the plot is more important than the characters. In melodrama the playwright shapes his characters to fit the plot. The characters are usually lacking in lifelike dimension. Macbeth is weak with no streak of strength that might enable him to save himself. Lady Macbeth is mean and vicious and has no redeeming virtues. The victims of their plot—King Duncan and Banquo—are noble and fine and do not have the mixture of good and bad that real people have.

These are the four fundamental forms of dramatic writing, but there are plays, and plays. There are plays that are well written and plays that are badly written. There are plays about history, science, business, industry, politics, and almost every subject one can think of. There are funny plays and sad plays, good plays and bad plays. Some contribute very definitely to that parental objection we mentioned above. They are a definite waste of time. Unfortunately, too many of this sort often get into the school drama program, and young people spend hours, days, and weeks rehearsing a kind of pulp that would never be tolerated in the English department. Such plays add nothing to the character development or to the talent development of anybody caught with such inferior material, but this can never be a legitimate argument against the importance of drama in the school. Again, a positive approach must be taken.

On the positive side is a wealth of great plays, plays that have stood the test of time, as well as new plays that have something significant to say and add to the cultural growth of all those who spend time with them. Spending time with great plays is like living with interesting, important people. Often the people in a play are like the kind of people we would like to be or become. Other times they are like people we would not like to emulate. Such characters point up by contrast certain qualities toward which we like to aspire. So the reading and rehearsing of great plays is like the study of great literature, except that it is better because we live with the characters through rehearsals and performances. It is this living with the characters and the ideas of a play that is the unique thing about drama. It is that experience that makes it different from other subjects and other activities.

Let us stress that word *experience*. It is a word that is basic to drama because it is through experience that we come to understand the remarkable world of drama, and it is though experience that we gain competence and confidence and move on toward our goal of excellence. We can read about drama, and we can read plays, but reading is not the same as doing. Reading this book for example, is not the same as putting into practice the pointers that are contained in the book. Merely reading this book, or any book about drama, is not going to turn anyone suddenly into a great star, or even a competent actor.

However, don't toss this book aside. Not yet. It may not contain a magic formula for immediate success, but it will give you much needed background for developing your talent. Background is essential in any art, and drama is an art. It is one of the oldest of the arts. It is as old as civilization itself, and even older.

Before we discuss just how old drama is, let us delve further into the various phases of drama. We have seen how plays are an indispensable aspect of drama. They are the textual material from which performances are produced. Let us now take a few paragraphs to explore the art of drama as it is expressed in performance.

When we say that drama is an art, we should add that

it is actually an art composed of several other arts. First there is the art of writing as evidenced in the play itself. Next there is the art of acting, which is essential to the performance of the play. Then there is the art of design as expressed in the stage settings, costuming, and lighting of the play. The arts of dance and music are often fused with the elements of performance. The art of architecture is present in the theatre in which the play is performed. Finally, there is the art that ties all the elements together into a total expression, which is the art of directing.

The performance is the product of all these basic arts. It is the end result of all the rehearsing, all the scene building, the making of costumes, the gathering of stage props. It is the presentation to the audience, and the audience itself becomes a part of the total event. The total event adds up to an experience in the theatre. That experience is a production.

While it is true that the production refers to the total experience, the word *production* has another connotation which we need to discuss. The term *production* often refers to the mechanical and technical aspects of a performance in contrast to the artistic phases. The building, mounting, and shifting of scenery, the gathering and making of props, the rigging and operating of lights and sound effects, and the borrowing or making of costumes all come under the general heading of production. On the other hand the acting, designing, and directing belong to the artistic phase of the performance.

The moment we begin to consider play production we become increasingly aware of the fact that there is much more to drama than acting. Acting is basic, of course, because if there were no actors to perform the play there would be little point to the other aspects of production. Nevertheless, the actors are only part of the production. For that matter, the play itself is but one part of the total production.

Let us now consider the mechanical and technical elements of a production. First let us recognize that it would be possible for a play to be presented without scenery, costumes, lighting, and even without props. Not only is it possible, but it is done quite frequently.

A classic example of this is the hundreds of Drama Trio performances which have been presented in colleges, schools, and churches from coast to coast. The Drama Trio, a touring unit from the University of Redlands, performs a repertoire of plays without scenery, costumes, or props. This simple and effective method of presentation has been copied extensively and the Trio plays have been done in England, Canada, South America, Japan, India, West Germany, and other nations. That the Drama Trio has performed in gigantic auditoriums such as Convention Hall in Atlantic City and the Coliseum in Portland, Oregon, and has done the same type of performance on a bare patch of earth by a Wisconsin lake, illustrates the fact that actors can perform with nothing but a play to work with. However, the arts of the theatre generally include more than a play and a group of actors. In this book, we are very much concerned with all the theatre arts and with the theatre itself. So, join us now in the theatre.

2

This is Theatre

Since a theatrical performance has to take place on a stage of some sort, let us first consider the various kinds of stages. Fundamentally a stage is merely that place where the actors present the play. It might be the end of a room, a corner of a patio, a section of a street, the chancel of a church, a designated segment of the gymnasium floor, or the platform of an auditorium. Wherever it is, the little patch of space in which the actors perform becomes a stage.

Back in the time of ancient Greece, the stage was at the bottom of a hill and the audience sat on benches in a semicircle carved out of the hill. During the time of Shakespeare, the stage was a raised platform with walls on three sides and a roof covering the stage only. The audience stood in an area that was open to the sky or sat in covered galleries at the rear and the sides. Shortly after Shakespeare's time, the proscenium stage became popular. Often referred to as the picture-frame stage, because the action is viewed through the frame of the proscenium arch, it continues to be the conventional stage of our time.

In our time, however, other types of stages have become popular. Foremost among these are the thrust stage and the center stage. The audience sits on three sides of a thrust stage, and on all four sides of a center stage. Another type recently made popular by Bernard Miles in his Mermaid Theatre on the banks of the Thames in London, is the open stage. The open stage is similar to a proscenium stage but has no curtain and no wings.

The curtain came with the advent of the proscenium stage and is still a handy device for dividing the stage from the audience. This curtain is called the house curtain or the act curtain, or sometimes the main curtain, to distinguish it from other curtains that are used from time to time as acting background. Background curtains are usually referred to as drapes or as a drape set. They are sometimes called traveler curtains because they travel on a track when they open and close. Sometimes a traveler curtain hanging halfway between the proscenium arch and the back wall of the stage is called the mid-main, but that is usually in a theatre where the house curtain is called the main curtain, especially in school auditoriums.

A fascinating tradition has grown up around the house curtain. Actors and audiences have developed a kind of reverence for "The Curtain," because it is the means of magic by which the wonderful world of make-believe is revealed and made to vanish. Everyone who has experienced that sinking feeling in the pit of the stomach when the curtain opens or rises, knows that special thrill of being on stage. Likewise everyone who has sat in the audience waiting excitedly for the curtain to rise knows the tingle of expectation.

If there is magic in the curtain, there is also magic in the wings. It is through the wings that the actors make their entrances and their exits, appearing and vanishing from the audience in that special enchantment which is drama. Shakespeare was keenly aware of this enchantment and made much of it, as is indicated in the following quotations:

Out, out, brief candle!
Life's but a walking shadow, a poor player
That struts and frets his hour upon the stage
And then is heard no more: it is a tale
Told by an idiot, full of sound and fury,
Signifying nothing.
Macbeth, act 5, scene 5

These our actors,
As I foretold you, were all spirits and
Are melted into air, into thin air.
The Tempest, act 4, scene 1

All the world's a stage,
And all the men and women merely players:
They have their exits and their entrances;
And one man in his time plays many parts,
His acts being seven ages.
As You Like It, act 2, scene 7

Actually, wings are merely segments of scenery which mask the off-stage areas, to the right and left, from the view of the audience. These segments may be draped fabrics which match the traveler curtain, in which case they are usually called leg drops, or the wings may be made of canvas flats. The term *flat* will be explained later for those unfamiliar with the term. These flats may be set up purely as masking units, or they may be erected to represent a wall.

Of course, there is more to a stage than curtains and wings. There is scenery, for instance. Many who have worked in productions may be aware of the fact that there are basically two kinds of scenery, soft and hard. The travelers and leg drops mentioned above, and all drape sets or scenery made of free-flowing fabrics would be considered soft scenery. Hard scenery consists of stairways, landings, window seats, platforms (called levels or risers), and any other structural pieces. Between the hard and the soft is the flat, which is a basic unit worthy of a paragraph all its own.

A flat is a unit of scenery made of canvas or heavy muslin stretched on a frame of lumber. The lumber used is usually one- by three-inch strips of soft pine wood. Each flat is equipped with hardware which makes it possible to lace a section of flats together to form a wall. Flats are held upright by stage braces attached to the flat and the stage floor. A full flat is usually about five feet six inches wide and from ten to fourteen feet high. Flats are painted according to the stage design that is called for and may represent either interior or exterior walls. Everyone interested in drama should make the acquaintance of a flat early in his career because it is a vital piece of modern scenery. Frequently tall folding screens are used in place of flats, but they are actually smaller flats hinged together.

Another piece of traditional scenery is the drop. The drop is also made of canvas or heavy muslin. Several widths of material are sewed together to make a large curtain that stretches across the stage from right to left and hangs from the top of the stage to the floor. By the top of the stage we mean the flies, which is another term soon to be explained. Ever since the time of the Renaissance, scenic artists have been painting drops to represent whatever is called for by way of background. This may range from a formal garden with fountains to a fairy-like woodland. Or the drop may be painted to represent a street, or a park, or merely the sky.

When a drop is not needed, it may be rolled up from the bottom or it may be flown into the flies. Of course, the latter can be done only when there is sufficient space in the stage loft to allow for lifting the drop out of view of the audience. In other words, the drop, when not in use, must be lifted so that it is concealed in the flies.

The flies is a rather loose term used to describe that area above the stage which is out of view of the audience.

The term probably comes from the fact that items of scenery are flown into the area for storage and, sometimes, for staging effects. The flies are masked by masking borders, running across the stage from right to left. These borders may be made of a fabric that matches the traveler curtain and leg drops, or may be made of canvas made to represent foliage or some other desired scenic effect. These borders usually hang from a pipe batten which can be raised or lowered by means of ropes and pulleys comparable to the rigging that handles the drops. Borders are raised or lowered to adjust to the set, but must serve to mask the flies from the audience.

Well-equipped stages have counterweight systems for the raising and lowering of drops, borders, leg drops, and all other items of scenery as well as lighting equipment that needs to be lifted into the flies. For example, the weight of a masking border is balanced by a series of iron pieces stacked in the counterweight arbor, much like the system by which a dumb waiter is operated. Each border or drop is attached to a pipe batten suspended by cables which run through pulleys in the ceiling of the stage (the grid), then attached to the counterweight which is off stage and out of view of the audience. Counterweights may be motor driven or manually operated.

An interesting bit of history is the fact that the old melodramas which were popular in this country during the last century were often presented in what was called a wing and drop set. The back drop might be painted to represent the interior of a log cabin, for example, with a door or a window cut out of the canvas. This was the back wall of the set. The sidewalls were not walls at all, but wings, or canvas flats, painted to look like the sides of the log cabin. However, they were not fastened together, but rather spaced so actors could enter and exit between them. Sometimes the scenic artist would paint a chair or some other piece of furniture on the wings, or paint in a fake staircase on the back drop.

From our discussion of scenery and stage mechanics we should go to a discussion of another important aspect of production, namely props, or properties. When is a prop a prop and when is it a piece of scenery? That is a question which even experienced theatricians sometimes have difficulty answering. If a set of stairs or a fireplace, or a built-in window seat is called for, is it a prop or not? No, it is not. None of these items actually come under the category of stage props. If they are attached to the set or built in, they are scenery. Furniture, on the other hand, is in the prop department. In fact, any item that is not attached to the scenery is a prop.

The difference between stage props and hand props may confuse beginners. Actually, the distinction is fairly simple. Items that are on the set at the beginning of a scene are stage props. This is true even if the items be small, such as pencils, ash trays, books, magazines, keys, etc. Properties that are carried on by the actors, even if they are the size of a trunk, are considered hand props.

There is also often confusion over props and costumes. Is a costume always a costume, or might it sometimes be considered a prop? Any costume is considered a prop when it is discovered on the set at the beginning of the act. Also any item of wearing apparel which is brought on stage wrapped in a package is a prop. A hat, or a raincoat, hanging on a rack when the play begins would qualify as a prop. A box which contains a suit which is carried on by an actor during the course of action is a prop even though the suit may later be worn by an actor. If this seems like a minor matter, we will discover later why it is important to clarify such things.

When we speak of costumes people sometimes imagine that term applies only to plays in which unusual clothes are worn. A Shakespearean play calls for period costumes. A fantasy like *Alice in Wonderland* calls for fanciful costumes. But a costume is any garment worn on stage by any actor. Cindy may wear her own party dress in the last act, but it is a costume while it is on the stage. It doesn't matter whether the clothes belong to the actors or not, or whether they are the latest fashion or of some historical period. On stage they are costumes.

Stage lighting and sound effects also being technical or mechanical elements of production, come next in our discussion. Let us take lights first. A long time ago plays were given only in the daytime, so the idea of stage lighting was unheard of. That was back in the time of the Greeks and Romans and during the Middle Ages when plays were given in cathedrals or church yards, or in the courts of castles. Then, as people became more sophisticated and started staying up late nights, they wanted nighttime entertainment, so actors began performing by candlelight. They used to line up a row of candles along the front of the stage (the apron), and put a plank in front of the candles to keep the light out of the eyes of the audience. These were the first footlights. Later, gas took the place of candles, and still later, shortly after Thomas Edison invented the incandescent light globe, electricity replaced gas.

With the advent of electricity theatres all over the civilized world lit up, and inventive technicians began doing fascinating things with stage lighting.

The very mention of stage lighting suggests two names with which we should be familiar. They are Gordon Craig and Adolph Appia. Both were stage designers who pioneered in the field of stage lighting. Both helped usher in the twentieth century with totally new approaches to the staging of drama.

Before the time of Craig and Appia, producers were satisfied with the old wing and drop type of scenery or with the so-called "box set" made up of flats laced together. Prior to their time, producers were also satisfied with flat lighting obtained from foot and border lights. Craig and Appia did away with drops and flats and foots and borders.

Gordon Craig started a trend in impressionistic scenery. His designs suggested an entire set by a mere portion of the set. A Gothic arch, for example, might suggest a cathedral, or a single pillar might suggest a Greek temple. Many of our modern designers still draw on the designs and writings of Gordon Craig for inspiration.

Adolph Appia believed, in contrast to Gordon Craig, that scenery and lighting should not detract from the actors. He sought to blend the lighting and the scenery with the action of the play. He used light to accent the plasticity of the human form. His scenery was designed to give the actor freedom of movement. In place of wings and drops he used dimensional pieces (units such as walls, doors, etc., that had thickness).

If you were a scene designer planning the sets for a realistic play such as one by Eugene O'Neill or Tennessee Williams, you might tend to follow Appia more than Craig. However, if you were designing sets for a Shakespearean play, you would be more inclined to get your ideas from Gordon Craig.

There was a Broadway producer named David Belasco back in the early part of the century who used to spend fortunes and hundreds of man hours creating such effects as sunsets through the use of stage lighting. Mr. Belasco was only one of many who experimented, with stunning results. Soon lighting became so important that companies went into business just to manufacture stage lighting equipment. Nowadays lighting is as much a part of a production as are the scenery and costumes.

When we stop to think about it, it is amazing to realize what can be done with light. Of course, the primary purpose of light on any stage is to illuminate the actors and the set. However, in addition to illumination, stage lighting can create mood, establish the time of day, and add color and accent to both actors and scenery. Lighting can do so much for a production that we should examine, briefly, the means by which the various lighting effects are achieved.

Basically there are two kinds of light in the theatre, diffused and concentrated. We have already mentioned footlights, which cast a diffused light. That is to say, the light spreads in all directions and illuminates everything within its range. Border lights and strip lights are also diffused. Border lights hang on battens in the flies and shine down on the heads, if not the faces, of the actors. Strip lights are similar to border lights but are used to cast light on a back drop from a position on the floor.

Floodlights are also diffused, but they give us a step in the direction of concentrated lighting. A floodlight is a rather large rectangular metal box in which a high wattage lamp is installed. Because the lamp is mounted inside the box the light which it casts comes from the open side of the box, thus giving some limited direction to the light. There are several kinds of floodlights, some with special names such as Olivette, Scoop, etc.

The concentrated lights are the spotlights. A spotlight resembles an ordinary flashlight in that it casts a concentrated beam in whatever direction the instrument is aimed. Basically there are two kinds of spotlights—one is soft-edged, the other sharp-edged. The first is created by a fresna lens, the latter by an ellipsoidal lens. There are variations and refinements of the two kinds of spotlights and they differ greatly in their wattage capacities, that is to say their candlelight power, but they are all used to put light specifically where it is wanted. With a series of spotlights, each area of the stage can be lighted separately. A shaft of light can be directed through a window from off stage, or down a stairs from the flies, or a spotlight may be used to accent some section of the stage. A movable spotlight, mounted in a booth or platform at the rear of the auditorium, can follow an actor about the stage. We need hardly add that this is called a follow spot.

We should include in the spotlight discussion the fact that there is an inexpensive spotlight on the market called the PAR which is often referred to as a display spot. In addition to being very inexpensive, it is self-contained. Other spotlights consist of metal cylinders with reflectors, lenses, and a special socket for mounting the spot globe. The PAR has its own reflecting device built into the globe, and it can be inserted into an ordinary house socket. Obviously its use is limited, since it cannot be focused down to a pinpoint or be spread to cover a large circumference, as is the case with standard spotlights, nor can the color be changed as in the regular spotlights. However, the PAR spots are available in various colors.

With the coming of electric lights to the theatre, came the means of changing color. In the early days, footlights and border and strip lights were wired in three or four circuits and each circuit serviced a different set of colors. One circuit controlled the white lights, another the red, another the blue, another the green, etc.

By controlling the volume of electricity which fed the circuits, it was possible to dim down any one circuit or combination of circuits, and thus mix the primary colors and produce a variety of colors. With the floodlights and the spotlights, however, it is possible to project virtually every color in the spectrum simply by changing the color medium. The color medium is a piece of translucent, fireproof material, of a given color, and contained in a metal frame which can be slipped in and out of a slot in front of the lens.

Along with color should be mentioned intensity. The magic of stage lighting is owing to the control of intensity as well as the control of color, shape, and direction. The sun can set, twilight descend, and night can fall by means of controlling the intensity of the various circuits.

At first there were only crude methods for controlling the intensity of light. A circuit was wired to a resistance dimmer, which was a coil made of wire that resisted electricity. Then came the dimmer, which was called the auto-transformer. This was followed with the magnetic dimmer, and today we have a type of dimmer known as the silicone control rectifier (solid state). The SCR dimmer can be controlled from a remote source. Thus it is possible to have a bank of dimmers somewhere in the backstage area and control those dimmers from a booth at the rear of the auditorium. This makes it possible for the operator of the lights to see what effects he is producing on the stage below.

Before turning from the mechanical to the artistic aspects of performance, we should discuss production organization. Who shifts the scenery? Who rustles props? Who operates the lights, etc.? Obviously someone has to be responsible for all these mechanical details, and this calls for organization. These important items cannot be left to chance, nor should they be left to the actors or the overworked director. The plan of organization may differ in different schools and in different theatres, but the following plan will serve as a fair example.

Naturally, the head of the organization is the director, because he is responsible for the production as a whole. In any sensible arrangement, authority and responsibility must go hand in hand. Whoever has a responsibility must have the authority to carry out that responsibility. However, being responsible for something doesn't necessarily mean doing it. It may, and often should mean merely seeing that the job gets done.

The director's right hand and handyman Friday is the stage manager. He helps the director at rehearsals by making certain that the actors are ready for their entrances, by getting the stage ready for rehearsals, and by writing into the prompt book the major directions which the director gives the actor. During the performance he is in complete command of everything backstage. He is in charge of opening or raising the curtain for the beginning of the play, and for closing or getting it down at the end of each act. He must make sure that the actors are ready for their entrances well ahead of their cues and that scenery and props get shifted quickly and efficiently. Sometimes the stage manager is also in charge of the production crews. However, this is a job that ought to be turned over to a technical director when at all possible.

The technical director is in charge of the mechanical aspects of the production. Under him are the various crews, which include building, painting, and stage (sometimes combined as the stage crew), properties, costumes, lighting, and sound. Sometimes members of the cast may serve on one or more of the crews, but actors with heavy roles should not be expected to engage extensively in crew work.

Crew work can be every bit as exciting as acting. This is evidenced by the fact that students often prefer working on a crew to taking a part in the cast. In any event, every actor should take his turn on a crew or two, just as everyone who works on a crew should take advantage of every acting opportunity that may come his way. Having a part in the play is only one facet in the drama experience. Anyone who limits himself only to acting or to crew work is missing the real thrill of being in drama.

Let us turn now to the artistic aspects of a performance. When we say that acting, designing, and directing are the artistic aspects, we are making a purely arbitrary division, because there can certainly be great artistry expressed in the preparation of scenery, costumes, light, sound, and even properties. These categories are merely a matter of convenience and should never suggest that the members of the crews are merely mechanics, while the members of the cast are the artists. Both are both, and all are engaged in the art of the theatre.

While acting is an art, there is much about it that is

purely technical. There is even much about acting that is mechanical, though it must never appear mechanical to an audience. Stage deportment, relaxation, breath control, diction, and projection are all aspects of acting that can be achieved only through technical control. As we analyze these aspects, we will see how mechanical they often seem to be.

Stage deportment refers primarily to the way an actor handles himself on stage. Young actors are often awkward and ill at ease and seem to have a positive genius for appearing at their worst. This is usually because of a lack of basic stage deportment. Once deportment is understood and put into practice, the inept actor becomes the competent actor.

Stage deportment has no other purpose than to show the actor at his best. We should begin with the simple recognition that an actor is on stage to be seen and heard by an audience. He may engage in acting as a kind of therapy or indulging self-expression, but that is not the kind of acting an audience comes to see.

There are certain conventions and traditional tricks that actors have passed on from generation to generation, and some of these conventions and tricks are phony and corny. However, the conventions that concern us are those that help the actor to look well and sound well.

How does he look well and sound well? In the first place, these are things he doesn't have time to think about when he is lost in a role. Therefore, he should know his theatre ABC's so well that he doesn't have to think about them. It should be second nature for him to move correctly and speak effectively. The ABC's he must master are as follows:

Right and left are from the actor's point of view as he faces the audience. In executing a direction to cross stage right, he crosses to his right. If the direction is stage left, he crosses to his left. Down stage is toward the audience, upstage is away from the audience. All stages, regardless of their size, are divided into six basic areas. Those areas are down right, down center, down left, up right, up center, and up left. Some directors like to subdivide these areas to include down right center, down left center, up right center, up left center, etc., but such variances are readily understood and need not complicate the issue. Directors sometimes refer to down right as "Right One," up right as "Right Three," and a position between the two areas as "Right Two." This numbering system naturally carries over to the center areas and the left areas. The numbering system immediately suggests stage planes, which may need some explanation. If four or five actors are standing in a straight line from down right to down left, they would all be in the same plane. If Actor A should step slightly upstage, he would be in a different plane. If Actor B stepped upstage slightly above Actor A he would be in still another plane. The positioning of actors in the different planes gives dimension to the stage picture. Actors should develop a sensitivity to planes, lest they become monotonous by playing constantly in the same plane with another actor. It is rudimentary stage technique for an actor to lead off with his upstage foot when he makes an entrance or crosses to another part of the stage. Likewise, he should kneel on his downstage knee and gesture preferably with his upstage hand. This keeps the actor's face and body open to the audience.

Now let the actor turn to the right and face the wings. Although he is presenting his left profile to the audience, he is standing in what is known as the right profile position. One slight turn to his left puts him in a one-quarter right position, another slight turn to his left puts him in a full front position, and still another to his left places him in a one-quarter left position. If he turns to the left and faces the left wings, he is in the left profile position. From the left profile position if he turns slightly to his left he will be in a three-quarter left position. If he turns slightly left again and presents his back to the audience he will be in a full back position. One more turn slightly to the left puts him in the three-quarter right position. The profile, three-quarter, and full back positions are known as the closed positions. The full front and one-quarter right and one-quarter left are called the open positions.

Actors should know the body positions and stage areas as thoroughly as a ball player knows the bases. Even a cub league rookie would never mistake first base for third, so a rookie actor should never mistake up right for down right or an open position for a closed one. An actor who doesn't know up from down or right from left is like a football player who doesn't know which goal to run for. So, just as a ball player has to become thoroughly familiar with a ball diamond or the field, so an actor must become familiar with the stage. He does this by spending time on a stage, either a real one or a pretend one in his room or in his dad's garage. As he practices going through the various body positions and crossing from one area to another, remembering always to take off with his upstage foot, these ABC's of the stage soon become second nature to him.

However, while Janey and John are practicing their ABC's, they should also practice keeping their heads up and their eyes and faces alert. An actor who stares at the floor and lets the audience see only the top of his head is certainly not very interesting for an audience to watch, and anything he has to say will probably not get past the footlights. Jane and John should also practice walking on the balls of their feet, holding their bodies erect and moving with purpose, dignity and grace.

John and Jane and all the others who want to become proficient in the rules of the game should also practice sitting and rising. It is an old theatrical trick for an actor to feel the chair or the sofa with the back of his leg and then sink gracefully to a sitting position with the weight on one leg, using the other leg for balance. He should also rise with the weight on one leg, and if he is to cross to another area immediatly, he should make certain that his weight is on his downstage foot. Along with this sitting technique we should consider the turning technique. If John is down right and wants to turn to face Jane, who is down left, he should turn with his feet as well as with his torso and head. This seems a natural enough thing to do, yet it is amazing how many young actors twist their bodies around as though their feet were firmly embedded in cement. An easy way to remember this technique is to bear in mind that nose and toes should generally point in the same direction.

When an actor moves from one area to another he is making a cross, or crossing. In a play script a direction to cross is usually indicated by an "X." Thus, the direction "UL x DR" would indicate that an actor who is standing up left is to cross to an area down right. Such a cross would be a diagonal cross, as would a cross from up right to down left. A cross from down right to down left or from up left to up right is a lateral cross. A cross from up right to down right, up center to down center, up left to down left, is considered a vertical cross. A cross from down left to up center to down right would constitute a curved cross, as would a cross from up right to down center to up left. Crosses that include a slight curve are generally more interesting and more graceful.

Let us now put John and Jane on stage and have them demonstrate how to share a scene. Let us put Jane up center and John up right. If they stand in those areas, both in the same plane, and talk to each other in profile positions, they are not likely to hold our interest more than a few seconds. Why? Because they would not be sharing the scene.

In order to share the scene, the actor who is speaking should be slightly upstage of the other, so that in addressing his partner he is playing with his face to the audience, or in an open position. In this case, let us say John is doing the talking and Jane is slightly downstage in a three-quarter right position looking at John. This makes it clear to the audience that John is the important person at that particular moment and Jane, the listener, is secondary. When John finishes speaking he might move a pace or two downstage and Jane, in turning to face him, would put herself in an open position so that she could command the scene. John could then assist her position of command by turning to face her, which would put him in a closed position. This, in essence, is what is meant by "sharing a scene." Naturally, actors should not be guilty of playing a game of teeter-totter with each other, but scene sharing, like all other acting techniques, must be done with subtlety, taste, and imagination.

In their demonstration of scene sharing, let us assume that John must cross from his position up right to the down left area. In doing this, he will pass between Jane and the audience. As he crosses in front of Jane, Jane should counter cross, which means a move in the opposite direction. As John moves stage left, Jane should move stage right. However, the counter cross need not and should not be broad and obvious. Stage movement should be ever so slight. It could even be nothing more than a turn of her body from a left profile to a right profile position. Nevertheless Jane, if she knows her acting fundamentals, will automatically make a counter movement when John or any other actor crosses either below her or above her.

In addition to the aesthetic value of the counter cross (it tends to keep the stage picture in balance) , it is a handy device for actors when they must move in order to keep from being blocked from view of the audience. An actor who is in an upstage position often finds himself blocked from the audience by an actor who has moved into a downstage position. It is the responsibility of the upstage actor to move into an area where he can be seen by the audience. This is especially important when an actor has a line that must be heard by the audience.

The designing of the stage movement and the positioning of the actors in the various groupings are the responsibility of the director, but the ability to execute the above skills should be up to each individual actor. The more skilled an actor is in these rudimentary techniques, the more he will save the director's time at rehearsals. The techniques we are discussing are both the rules of the game and the tricks of the trade. They are to the actor what a knowledge of the game is to the athlete.

This is a good place to point out that there are sometimes exceptions to the rules we have been discussing. Take the rule regarding sitting and rising, for example. When an actor is playing a character who flops on sofas or flops himself into a chair, he would naturally disregard the rules. Or if a situation calls for characters shuffling along an icy sidewalk, they would hardly be expected to bound about erectly on the balls of their feet. Character interpretation always enters into the way in which the rules are used, but it is imperative to note that the rules should be known, and be known thoroughly, before they can be intelligently broken.

Thus far, the rules have dealt mostly with the visual aspects of acting; let us turn now to the voice. What are the rules for helping the actor sound well? What does it mean to sound well? The answer can be summarized in one word—communication.

An actor must communicate with his audience. To be sure, he can communicate quite extensively on the visual level. In fact, he can project a lot of ideas and provoke many thoughts purely through pantomime, but if he has words to speak, he must speak them with clear communication.

His objective is twofold—to be heard, and to be understood. In order to be heard, he must project. This does not mean yelling or shouting. All too often, young actors make the mistake of shouting their lines. This often results in inarticulate noise and a sore throat. Simply expressed, projection is a matter of getting the voice up and out so that it can be heard throughout the auditorium. It is a matter of breathing deeply and speaking on the breath. It is a matter of giving the conversational voice enough volume to make it carry to the back row.

At a ball game, or on the playing field, students have no trouble projecting. Even the shy ones are able to communicate from home base to center field or from one end of the tennis court to the other. Oddly enough, those same students on stage are likely to mumble so they can't be heard even in the first row. The obvious trick, then, is to apply to the stage the vocal technique that is used in the athletic field. The trick is to breathe and let out the voice. The trick is to talk to the person in the back row as you would talk to the friend on the oppsite end of the playing field.

The trick, too, is to remember that acting on the stage is not life. It must be bigger than life. Dialogue should sound like conversation, but it is not the same as a private conversation because it has to be heard by the public.

Naturally, it is not enough to be heard. You must be understood. This means you must speak with clear diction and comprehension. Diction consists of pronouncing the words correctly and with clean articulation. Pronunciation and articulation sometimes involve ear training. Often vowels are distorted and consonants are slurred because the speaker has never listened to himself very carefully. Listening to oneself on a tape recorder can be very helpful. However, listening should be supplemented with diction drills such as will be found later in this book.

Being understood also involves a comprehension of what is being spoken. You cannot make others understand something that you yourself do not fully understand. Merely speaking lines that you have memorized by rote is not communicating. At least, it is not communicating unless you comprehend what it is that you are trying to communicate. An actor must know the meaning of his lines before he can speak them with meaning. Therefore, it is not enough for him merely to memorize his words. He must understand the moods and inner motivations of the character he is portraying. He must study more than lines. He must study the character, and above all he must study the entire play.

Return now from rudimentary acting techniques to the principles of design. Here our discussion will be limited and elementary, because we are treating design merely as one of the arts of the theatre with which junior high school students should have some acquaintance. Students at the intermediate level are usually more interested in acting and stagecraft than they are in designing and directing.

It may be sufficient to say that the best design is one which does not call attention to itself. This is true of scenery, costumes, and lighting. However, this does not mean that a designer cannot be artistically effective. On the contrary, he can express great artistry, but his objective is always to enhance the play. His stage settings must not only provide the locale for the play, with entrances and exits placed in the most advantageous positions, but they must project the period, mood, and atmosphere of the play. The setting must suggest at once the nature of the play and the kind of people who are to be seen in the play.

What is true of the setting is equally true of the costumes and lighting. All must contribute to the playwright's intent and the director's concept. All must contribute and nothing must distract. Each costume must be right for the period and must be true to the social and economic status and the emotional integrity of the character. The lighting must not be a series of effects for the sake of effects, but must blend with the mood and help to tell the story of the play.

The designer begins by reading the play many times. He will also no doubt have several conferences with the director. In fact, he should know the director's concept and his basic pattern of movement before he goes too far with his designing. He must know where the director wants his entrances and exits, where he may want stairs and landings, window seats and fireplaces, etc. Knowing these things, the designer then makes a few preliminary sketches, and when they are approved by the director, he makes renderings in color and then produces a set of working drawings. The designer follows through by supervising the crews and making certain that they come as close as possible to creating the settings, costumes, and lighting which he has designed.

We should also treat briefly the director's art, for the reasons stated above. Although the director's art is worthy of the many books that have been written about it, it can be sketchily summarized and still be presented as the significant aspect of theatre that it naturally is.

It can be safely said that much of the director's work is already behind him by the time the play goes into rehearsal. This is because he must spend many hours reading many plays in order to select one for production. Having made his selection, he then spends many hours studying the text of that play and doing whatever research is necessary to make the play ready for production. Furthermore, he has been through the period of tryouts and casting and has no doubt had conferences with all those who will be helping with the production. He has also done his homework on the script and has the blocking of the stage business fairly well in mind before he goes into rehearsal.

By blocking is meant the movement of the actors in terms of their entrances and exits, their crosses from area to area, when they sit and when they stand, and what particular detailed business they will engage in. Once he has roughed in the blocking, he will begin to work for character development on the part of the actors and detailed business designed to delineate the characters. As a part of his art he will make sure that each and every stage picture is well composed in respect to the elements of composition and that he is telling the story of the play through movement and picturization. He will listen carefully for line readings and try to make certain that each character is projecting his role with honesty and effectiveness, and he will do whatever coaching is necessary to achieve that end. He will listen also for the orchestration of voices and help his actors achieve the necessary vocal variety. Finally, he will blend actors, scenery, costumes, properties, lighting, and sound into an artistic whole.

Throughout the production adventure, he, or more likely she, will have met many crises, worked out a score of alternatives, ridden herd on the crews, served as mentor, psychiatrist, and father confessor to members of the cast, and when it's all over, be ready to head for a vacation in Bermuda. However, there is no Bermuda. There is only business as usual come Monday morning. For the school director, there are classes to teach, papers to grade, scenery to strike, properties to return, grades to make out, and the next production.

The preceding pages have presented both a grandstand view of drama and a backstage look at theatre arts. The view and the look are far from comprehensive. There is more to see and more to learn. The more we see of drama the more fascinating it becomes. The more we learn of theatre arts the more we seem to want to learn. This is only natural, because drama is like life. It is a mirror held up to nature, as Shakespeare put it. Drama is so important to life that people have been putting on plays and going to see plays ever since the human race began. In the next chapter we will explore the effects of drama on the human

race and see how it has both reflected and helped to fashion the various civilizations. Before we begin that exploration, there is a fact to face, a fact that has to do with drama
today.

The fact is this. Today is a time of rapid change. There
is nothing new about change. Change is the story of evolution. However, in our time, things seem to change faster
and more frequently than ever before in the history
of man.

Because we live in this period of changing tides, we must
learn to ride the tides. We need to keep ourselves sensitive
and on the alert. We have to be ready to accept and sometimes even to initiate change. On the other hand, we have
to be capable of rejecting change when it is not in the best
interest of human progress. We have to keep in mind that
all change is not necessarily good. We need to distinguish
between the latest and the best. There is a popular notion
to the effect that if a thing is new it is good. Such is not
the case, necessarily.

As we become responsible citizens, we have to make
judgments. In fact, the making of judgments is part of the
process of becoming a responsible citizen. In drama as in
life we must make judgments. Today's drama, like everything else, is undergoing change. Some of the change is
good. Some is bad. How do we know which is which? How
do we make sound judgments? The answer is not, as the
ballad has it, "blowing in the wind." The answer is in enlightenment, the kind of enlightenment that comes from
a knowledge of our heritage. Not all conventions and traditions of the past are relevant to contemporary life, but we
can judge their relevance only when we know them. The
more we know about our heritage, the better we will be
able to select and retain those things that are good about
it, and the more we can intelligently disregard those things
that are passé. So, like a Balboa exploring the New World,
let us now explore our heritage.

3

This is How It All Began

Then there was Thespis, the first actor. That was in Greece, some 500 years before Christ. But was there really a man named Thespis, and was he the first actor? Maybe yes and maybe no. There was in ancient Greece an entertainer, a teller of tales, a man who reenacted old legends, and his name may have been Thespis, but he was not the first actor.

Ages and ages ago, around some primitive campfire, a chieftain may have told the story of a hunt in dances and pantomime. Others soon joined in to give the story action and dialogue, and a primitive form of drama came into being. Where and when that was, nobody knows, but it may have happened in several places simultaneously. Like the child who instinctively imitates a cat, a dog, a parent, or any living thing in sight, man in the childhood of the race imitated the life around him. His imitating soon became a kind of ritual, like a prayer for rain or a paean of thanksgiving. In primitive and in ancient times, drama was a part of man's religion. We need only study the customs of primitive tribes in the world today to get a glimpse of what things were like when men were primitive everywhere. The *homo sapiens* tribes have not evolved with any marked degree of uniformity. Thus, it is possible to study primitive drama among the primitive peoples of our time.

It is also possible to study primitive drama in our own back yards if there are children playing there. Observe a group of youngsters as they play, and you will quickly see how they enter spontaneously into one role after another. They are not performing for an audience but their play takes on the primary aspects of drama. Later, if encouraged, they will perform for others, and so present a kind of drama in evolution.

Through the lost centuries of eons past, the evolution of drama went on, and as civilization evolved, the art of drama evolved. All through the millenniums of ancient Egypt drama was in evidence. It was a feature of the celebrations to the gods. The Egyptian plays were great spectacles of pageantry in which fierce mock battles were fought. Actually, the battles were not entirely mock. Human life being of little value to the Pharaohs, actors playing soldiers were often slain. Many of these plays, called Pyramid plays, have been handed down to us and are available in translation.

When the legendary Thespis came to Athens, something new came with him. That thing that was new is singular because it distinguishes the East from the West. The Pharaohs of Egypt built pyramids. The free people of Greece built theatres. Pyramids are tombs for the dead. Theatres are temples for the living. In Egypt, as in all the oriental civilizations, life for the most part was a miserable affair, and death, it was thought, was an entrance to a better existence. In Greece, life was a thing to be lived to the fullest, and to the Greeks their games, their drama, their art, their architecture, their politics, were all indispensable means to the abundant life. The fog of doom and gloom veiled the superstitious East. The Greeks walked proudly in the pure sunlight of reason.

Out of that reason came the first democracy, the beginning of the Olympics, and the greatest drama the world had ever known. Out of that age of reason came science, philosophy, and the theatre. For the Greeks, the theatre was a place to worship and to laugh. In Athens everyone went to the theatre, rich and poor, young and old. The days of the plays were holidays, and the drama contests were joyous festivals.

The contests were held each year in honor of Dionysus, god of fertility, and later god of the drama. Prizes were awarded the best plays and the best actors, and honors heaped upon all who participated in the production. All of the participants were citizens active in the life of the community. Many of them were athletes, soldiers, and politicians. Many of them were artists, musicians, dancers, poets, and philosophers. With the Greeks, the arts were a mark of masculine virility quite as much as games. A youth might sculpt, paint, write poetry, and act and dance in the dramas, and be a champion in the Olympic games. Among the youths of Athens the talk was of sports and poetics, games and drama, fun and philosophy, champions and politicians, and, no doubt, girls.

Girls, or at least women, enjoyed a great deal of feminine freedom during the heyday of Athens. They did not act in the plays. Acting was a man's activity. But they danced and sang and played musical instruments, and they too talked of many things, including boys, undoubtedly.

Out of this golden age of the world's first democracy emerged four giants whose names should be familiar to everyone interested in drama. They are Aeschylus, Sophocles, Euripides, and Aristophanes. The first three were writers of tragedy, the fourth one of the most famous authors of comedy—contest winners, all. There were other Athenian playwrights, of course—many of them. But these are the ones whose work has come down to us. Unfortunately many of their plays have been lost, but the samples of their works that are extant are gems of drama that are still frequently produced.

Aeschylus was the first of the Greek tragedians, and he

made his entrance around 495 B.C., shortly after the Greeks had beaten back the hordes of Persians who had attempted an invasion. It is thought that Aeschylus himself had a part in the working of that military miracle while serving his time in the Athenian army. This was about forty years after Thespis came to town, but Thespis was a solo actor, performing only with a chorus. Using masks to distinguish the different characters, Thespis played all the parts himself. The chorus, which was always an integral part of Greek plays, provided background, established locale, and created atmosphere through dance, song, and the spoken word. When Aeschylus came along, he added a second actor. With two actors the action became more exciting, and drama took on a more definite form.

It may be that Aeschylus introduced not one but two additional actors, but he is remembered for something much more important than that. His real gift to tragedy was content and style, a profound insight into religious concepts, and a magnificent and poetic treatment of human suffering. The stark, simple verse of his tragedies was more moving than anything that had yet been written.

This father of the classical tragedy wrote between 70 and 90 plays in all before his death in 456 B.C. Unfortunately, only seven of his plays are in existence today. They are *Agamemnon; The Libation Bearers; The Furies; The Suppliants; The Persians; Prometheus Bound;* and *The Seven Against Thebes.*

The real prize-winner was Sophocles, who between 471 and 405 B.C. wrote 100 plays, won 18 first prizes, and never dropped below second place in any of the annual contests. He was as perceptive as he was prolific, and his tragedies demonstrated his concern for the passions, catastrophes, vagaries, and misfortunes of his fellow man. Sophocles wrote with great compassion. To him, human suffering was not punishment by the gods for some sin committed, but rather an experience through which men developed strength of character. The tragic figures of his plays rose above their suffering in a kind of spiritual exaltation. His heroes, though defeated, experienced a kind of heroic triumph through acceptance and serenity.

Sophocles has been called the author of pure tragedy. Certainly, he was pure Greek in that he championed the dignity of the individual and saw nobility in man's existence. These are the virtues for which he is remembered, although it should be added that Sophocles engaged still another actor in the performing of his plays. His plays were always performed with three actors and a chorus. It must be remembered, of course, that each actor played several of the roles, including the feminine ones.

There are also only seven of Sophocles' plays in existence. They are *Antigone; Electra; Oedipus Rex; The Women of Trachis; Ajax; Philoctetes,* and *Oedipus at Colonus.*

Euripides, who lived from 484 to 406 B.C., was the playwright who jumped the generation gap. He was the young people's poet. He was the rebel, the critic of the Establishment. Naturally, he was not very popular with the older generation, but the young people loved him. Of the 92 plays he wrote, only five won prizes. But he felt a kind of victory in his defiance of the conventional gods. He was fearless in his criticism of both heroes and gods, and his fearlessness was reflected in the courageous action of his characters.

As we read or see his plays today, we realize that Euripides was trying to give his characters psychological motivation long before the word "psychology" had been invented. This is why his characters seem more realistic to us than do the characters of Aeschylus and Sophocles. Being something of a skeptic, he did not share Sophocles' noble opinion of mankind, and did not hesitate to reveal man's foibles in highly dramatic situations. Situations were important to him and that is why his plays seem to have more

conflict and more action than do those of his contemporaries.

Like many a prophet before and since, Euripides was
ahead of his time. However, soon after his death his name
came to be revered and his plays became popular. Nevertheless, his plays have not stood the test of time in quite
the same way that the plays of Aeschylus and Sophocles
have. This is probably because his plots are a little too
contrived and his characters and language are not suffi-
ciently majestic.

The plays of Euripides that are extant include *Alcestis;
Medea; The Children of Heracles; Hippolytus; Cyclops;
Hecuba; Andromache; The Madness of Heracles; The
Suppliant Women; Ion; The Trojan Women; Iphigenia
in Tauris; Electra; Helen; The Phoenician Women;
Orestes; The Bacchantes;* and *Iphigenia in Aulis.*

The tremendous gift of Greece to the Western world
cannot be fully measured, but the greatness of Greece and
the significance of her contribution to Western civilization
is thrillingly reflected in the plays of her three great
tragedians. In the theatre of ancient Greece men and
women gathered together in a communion of exaltation.
They experienced universal suffering and universal re-
joicing as the actors spoke not so much to them as for them.
The plays were based on oft-told tales, myths about heroes
and gods that Homer sang of 800 years B.C. Old tales re-
told, old adventures reenacted, were a part of the culture
that was to shape the culture of the Western world. Surely
an aspect of that culture was the Greek's remarkable
capacity to weep and his equally remarkable capacity to
laugh. Laughter is the cue for Aristophanes. Let us make
way for his entrance.

We are seated with our friends not far from the stage,
under the blue Athenian sky. It is late afternoon, and we
are drying our eyes from the last of the three tragedies
composing the trilogy that began early this morning. Every-

one in the huge, crowded amphitheatre is silent. All of us feel the impact, the beauty, and the power of what we have just witnessed. Now a murmur stirs like a breeze across the crowd and people all around us begin to talk with increased excitement as they anticipate the last play of the day, the comedy.

It is a comedy by Aristophanes. Aristophanes. Who else? Once more, he is author of the prize-winning play, the one we are about to see. Others enter plays, and others sometimes win, but Aristophanes is our favorite.

There were comedies before Aristophanes began to write. There were short, comical skits called satires. Historically, they came before the comedies, and, like the comedies, were presentd at the end of the long day's program when the tragedies were over. But now we are in the time of great comedy, the time of Aristophanes. Aristophanes! We have to grin from ear to ear each time his name is mentioned. Aristophanes, the favorite.

He's known all over Athens. He's known and loved by nearly everyone. He's loved by that market-place philosopher, Socrates. Socrates, the old gadfly, always has a crowd of youths and intellectuals trailing him about. Socrates and his endless questioning always in search of truth! "Know thyself," he says; "therein lies all wisdom." No doubt his sharp wit is a whip to Aristophanes. It may be that that gives the sting to the comedies of Aristophanes.

It is the sting that makes his comedies different. No doubt of that. Other writers of comedy can be funny. But there is a special bite to the plays of Aristophanes. His characters make us laugh, then make us wonder sometimes why we laughed. His lines will roll us in the aisle with laughter, then make us sit up and think twice.

This funny fellow lampoons everything in sight. He's absolutely fearless in his spoofing. He'll spoof the government and city officials. He'll make us see how stupid and ridiculous war is, then turn around and make us laugh at pacifists. He'll ridicule the women and end up praising them. He'll ridicule the gods, philosophers, and poets. He'll ridicule and rib and spoof us all and even make the playwrights look silly.

The chatter all around us turns to laughter now as huge comical birds fill the orchestra. We know at once they are not real birds. They are too large, and their plumage too outlandish. They are the chorus of the comedian's latest play, *The Birds*. The colorful costumes and comic gestures of the chorus are balanced by the beauty of the poetry sung and spoken. Two or three actors play out the boisterous action of the play, barking out the witty dialogue which is sometimes directed to selected members of the audience.

A while ago we wept from pity and from awe as we watched the tragedy. Now we weep with laughter. We weep and shake and hold our sides and all too soon the comedy is finished. Reluctantly we leave, and with the great dispersing crowd, we feel how good, how great it is to be Greeks in the golden age of Athens.

All that was long before the Puritans and the quaint Victorian standards. Puritans are shocked at Aristophanes. So are those still influenced by Victorian standards. His jokes are often bawdy, and his laugh lines hit below the belt. But to the free, life-loving Greeks, there was nothing unnatural or obscene in the fresh and candid comedies. Nor was there any censorship. The Athenians had a mutual trust in taste, good sense, and common decency. They believed in freedom, and had no fear that freedom would turn into irresponsible license, because each citizen felt his responsibility toward freedom.

Plays authored by Aristophanes include *The Banqueters; The Acharnians; Thesmophoriazusae; The Frogs; The Knights; The Clouds; The Wasps; Peace; The Birds; Lysistrata; Women in Parliament; Plutus; Aeolosicon;* and *Cocalus.*

There was in that time of great, exciting theatre an almost perfect balance of mind and spirit. Men searched their souls for truth and beauty and disciplined their minds to live by reason. Life was real and rough, and sometimes violent and ugly, but its goal was the joy of fulfillment. Freedom was a thrilling adventure, but the wise Greeks knew that there could be no freedom without responsibility.

The wise Greeks knew that. Wise people in all ages know it. But there came a time when Athens lost its wise men, and the foolish men who imagined they could rule by might fell heir to Athens and to all of Greece. Soon the Hellenic dream of conquest and expansion was matched by the conquest and expansion by a man from Macedonia named Alexander the Great.

The Macedonians mastered the Greeks, but the Greek spirit lived a while longer to spread throughout the Alexandrian world. That spirit continued to inspire the building of theatres and the performing of plays. There was a difference. Interest in the great tragedies waned, and a new kind of comedy replaced the old comedies of Aristophanes. The old comedy was a product of a free people. The subjects of Alexander were no longer free. No writer of new comedy dared poke fun at his government or advocate change.

One name should be remembered in connection with the new comedy. It is the name of Menander, an Athenian who wrote 100 plays, only one of which has survived, and that one only recently discovered.

Meanwhile, from the West, the shadow of Rome grew longer as it stretched across the decaying Grecian culture. Rising to power in the third century B.C., Rome gradually discovered Greek drama, and, after conquering what was left of Greece, began to call the plays and the players. At first both the plays and the players were Greek. The players were now the slaves of the Romans and the plays were quickly Romanized.

It would be quite wrong to assume that the Romans never heard of drama until they captured Greece. Through the centuries the Romans and the peoples of Sicily engaged in play-making as a part of their religious rituals and as a feature of their holiday festivals. However, Rome's chief gift to drama lay in her talent to adapt the Greek plays to the Roman culture. The Roman taste for tragedy was diminished by her hunger for comedy. The Romans had a few comedy traditions that blended happily with the Grecian concept of comedy. There had been comedies in Sicily as far back as 500 B.C. Primarily it was a comedy of ridicule, so it was only natural that the Romans would develop a comedy of parody and burlesque.

The champions of the Roman comedy were Plautus and Terence. They dropped the Grecian chorus entirely and wrote plays that were stronger in plot than those of the early Grecian writers. The comedies of Plautus and Terence were popular about 205–160 B.C. Twenty plays by Plautus have come down to us, but we have only six by Terence.

The plays of Plautus are farcical in nature and often include singing and dancing. The plays of Terence are more like domestic sentimental comedies. Unlike Aristophanes, neither of these playwrights engaged in political lampooning.

While the Romans were known best for comedy, they did have some serious drama. They, like the Greeks, had festivals and contests, but instead of honoring the god Dionysus, whom they called "Bacchus," they liked to honor all their gods and they enjoyed doing it as often as possible. It seems they seized upon any excuse for a Roman holiday. Sprinkled among the holiday comedies were always a few tragedies.

One writer of Roman tragedy should be remembered. His name was Lucius Annaeus Seneca. He was born about four years before the coming of Christ and died in 60 A.D.

His plays were modeled on the tragedies of the Greeks, and his favorite seems to have been Euripides. Of his nine plays that have come down to us, five of them are based on plays by Euripides.

Seneca is important to us not because he wrote great plays, but rather because his plays appear to have had a strong influence on the playwrights who would emerge some fifteen hundred years later. We must remember that it was the rediscovery of Greek and Roman manuscripts that helped to bring about the Renaissance. Shakespeare, a giant of the Renaissance, may have studied the plays of Seneca when he was a boy in the public school at Stratford-on-Avon. In any event, some of his plays do show the influence of Seneca.

There is a curious thing about this Lucius Annaeus Seneca. He was not really a playwright by profession at all. Nor is there any evidence that any of his plays were ever produced. Actually, he was a kind of court adviser to the emperor. That position must have taken a great deal of time because the emperor was none other than Nero, and Nero had problems.

One of Nero's problems was Christians. There were a number of them in Rome during that first century A.D., and they didn't like Nero and they didn't like his kind of theatre. Nero's idea of a thrilling, hilarious show was to put a few Christians into a cage with a hungry lion. Nero figured that if he gave the people a little bread and entertainment exciting enough to keep their minds off their troubles, he could go on ruling indefinitely. The Christians, forced to meet secretly in the catacombs of Rome, had other ideas. You might say they were subversive.

It was no wonder that the Christians developed a decided distaste for the Roman entertainment in the theatre as well as the arena. In the theatre, the comedies poked fun at the Christians and ridiculed their sacraments. Furthermore, the comedies were licentious, vulgar, and depraved, and were a far cry from the lusty, candid criticism expressed in the plays of Aristophanes.

Caesar Nero was to the first-century Christians what Adolf Hitler was to the twentieth-century Jews, yet another Caesar would one day embrace Christianity and Rome would become the official center of Christendom for centuries to come. Ironical? Yes. Ironical, too, is the fact that Christianity, the one-time enemy of the theatre, would be responsible for the resurrection of drama long after the death and decay of ancient Rome.

From the land beyond the Alps the barbarians came down to conquer and to plunder, and as the splendor of Rome faded in twilight the theatres blacked out and the actors took to the roads. The roads eventually led into nearly every part of Europe. The actors became troupers, traveling from town to town, from courtyard to courtyard, playing for pennies, playing for nothing, playing for a scrap of bread. Troubadours, dancers, acrobats, magicians —they became jacks of all arts and masters of improvisation. They, and their descendants, trouped their way into Spain, Portugal, France, Scandinavia, Germany, the British Isles, and even into Russia. Vagabonds and showmen, befriended and bedeviled, they trouped the trails for a thousand years and kept the ancient art of the theatre barely alive until religion reclaimed her wayward daughter.

The wayward daughter still went her way on the backs and pack mules of the wandering players, but with the building of great cathedrals the Christian church began to do what the Greeks and Romans and the Egyptians had done in earlier centuries. In earlier times important religious events were reenacted. The faith that bound the people together was dramatized in plays. The gods and heroes of distant times were made to walk the stages of the present. So tenth-century Christianity began to resurrect its saints and martyrs and tell the story of the Gospel through the power of the drama.

From the tenth century into the Renaissance the church enjoyed five hundred years of drama patronage. For those 500 years the Christian church was the foremost sponsor of drama in the Western civilized world. Thousands of plays involving tens of thousands of people were presented in cathedrals and churches throughout Christendom. Clergymen became playwrights, priests became players, and virtually every Bible story from the Creation to Revelation was dramatized and produced. Sometimes the plays took many days to perform. Sometimes the cast included hundreds of laymen. Usually, the dramas were presented on holy days. It was a means for reaching the masses. We should remember that in those days few people could read and write, but they could all see and hear, and feel the impact of the drama.

These mystery, miracle, and morality plays, as they were called, became so popular that the churches could not contain the congregation. As a result the dramas were often presented on the steps of the cathedral or in the village square. Later they were presented on huge pageant wagons that were drawn about from village to village. The parish craftsmen took on the responsibility for these pageant wagons, and guilds of craftsmen similar to our labor unions vied in friendly competition.

The wagons moved in cycles, traveling from village to village or from one part of the town to another. It went something like this: Wagon One, containing appropriate scenery for the first play of the cycle, would move into Station A and the actors would present the play to the crowd assembled at Station A. Then Wagon One would move to Station B to repeat its play for the B crowd and Wagon Two, containing scenery for the second play in the cycle, would replace Wagon One at Station A and proceed with its performance. Meanwhile, Wagon Three, containing scenery for the third play of the cycle, would be standing by, and when Wagon One moved on to Station C and Wagon Two moved to Station B, Wagon

Three would take its place at Station A and the last play of that particular cycle would be performed. This system made it possible for many people in different locations to see the performance of the complete cycle all in the course of a single day.

Of the thousands of plays that were written for the medieval church, only a few have been preserved. Judging from those plays that are extant, none can compare with the great tragedies of Greece. Nevertheless, most of them are moving, and some are highly amusing. Amusing? Is that surprising? It might be, if we think of religion as something lugubrious and super-solemn. The writers of the cycle plays had a sense of humor, and they discovered something that the Greeks and Romans never learned. They discovered that comedy and tragedy could be fused together in one play, and that comedy could be used to heighten tragedy. This was a discovery that Shakespeare would bring to full fruition in another century or two.

As the drama gradually left the church and took to the streets, more and more comedy was added. As the guilds replaced the clergy as the sponsors, the plays became more secular. The evolution was in process, an evolution that would lead straight to the advent of Shakespeare and his contemporaries. Meanwhile, let us not forget those traveling troupers. They were aiding in the evolution. They were the competitors of the clergy and laymen who presented the church plays and of the amateurs who appeared in the cycle plays. But together they were preparing for another great era of drama, the greatest since the time of Greece—some think even greater. We are speaking, of course, of the Renaissance and the Elizabethans. So, let us turn to the next chapter and open the curtain on that fabulous wonderland, the Renaissance.

4

This is How It Grew and Grew

As you read this book does it occur to you that you may be a person of importance in a new movement of great significance? Such an idea may not have entered the heads of those teenagers reading books in a little school in Stratford, England, back in the sixteenth century. Nevertheless, one of those teenagers would one day become one of the most famous men in history. Nobody knew it then, but the boy who answered to "Willie Shakespeare" would stretch his name through the centuries and into every corner of the civilized world. William Shakespeare—his fame is almost too great to fathom. Yet in the time of his early teens he could not know that he was already a part of a great important movement.

That movement is known now as the Renaissance, but nobody at the time thought of calling it anything special. In fact, many people didn't know that anything special was going on. Certainly the buddies of young Will Shakespeare chasing rabbits on the banks of the Avon River, teasing the swans, and filching fruit from the farmers, saw nothing special in the time or even in their friend, young Will.

The fascinating thing about history is that we are making it all the time and are scarcely aware of it. Although we may not know it, we may be part of a movement much more remarkable than the Renaissance. In fact, it seems quite evident that we are living in an extraordinary period. Are we a part of it? Of course. We cannot escape. However, the importance of our part is a point to ponder. While we ponder on the part we might be playing in some present renaissance, let us feel our way into that other Renaissance.

It did not happen overnight. We might expect a renaissance to happen suddenly, but it never does. A renaissance is a great awakening. It is a kind of rebirth of mankind at its best. For such an earthshaking event there must be preparation.

There was preparation all through the Middle Ages. In England, France, Italy, Spain, and everywhere in Europe, men were in search of something better than the miserable existence most of them endured. Christian crusaders with motives not altogether Christian journeyed to Palestine. A prince in Italy named Marco Polo traveled to China and made contact with the civilization of Genghis Khan. Then, as now, travel broadened the mind of the traveler, and fostered an exchange of cultures as well as goods.

Of course, the world was small and flat in those dark times. Anyone who doubted that was branded "heretic." The world was flat, and practically nobody doubted that. Ignorance is always hard to shake and all the brilliant learning of the ancient Greeks and Romans was long forgotten. Yet there were heretics who dared defy the ignorance, and there were scholars who searched for wisdom of the past.

In the fifteenth century everybody knew that the sun went around the earth, everybody but Nickolaus Copernicus (1473–1543). He proved that the earth goes around the sun. For that, he was called a heretic. A century later people still clung to the ancient notion that the moon was a luminous disc, but along came a musician and artist named Galileo. "Not so," said Galileo. What did a painter of pictures and a player of the organ and lute know about the moon? It happened that Galileo was also a scientist. He presented scientific proof that the moon was a sphere like the earth and gave off light only reflected from the sun. For that he, too, was branded heretic. Even in those distant times young geniuses had problems with the Establishment.

The earth, which had been spinning about its business in the solar system for unknown centuries, gradually expanded and took shape in the imaginations of men. As scholars learned more about civilizations of the past, they shared their knowledge, and the more the people learned the more excited they became about the idea of learning. Now it was revealed to the masses of the West that there had once been such things as science, art, philosophy, and great drama; and people, especially the young, were impatient to have those things again. From the navigating Vikings in the north came stories of a vast new land across the western sea, and in 1492 Columbus found that land. He found it quite by accident. He was on his way to India. Thus the age of exploration contributed to the new awakening.

In Italy, Leonardo da Vinci painted masterpieces and dreamed the impossible dream. He sketched the dream. It was a drawing of a machine that would fly in the air. In England Sir Francis Bacon wrote brilliantly of new scientific discoveries. In Germany, a man named Gutenberg invented the printing press. With it came books and pamphlets and an end to mass illiteracy.

All this was part and parcel of the Renaissance. In fact, it was the Renaissance. It was the age of intellectual awakening, the age of new discovering, and the age of man's rediscovery of man. Man saw himself as an individual. Man saw himself as a free agent, with purpose, dignity, and responsibility. He felt free to grow and learn, free to try his hand at anything and everything, and his goal was versatility and excellence. To excel, to do all things well—that was the responsibility of the real Renaissance man.

Such a man was William Shakespeare, poet, actor, playwright, producer, man of affairs, and citizen of England in the time of Good Queen Bess. The good queen, Elizabeth I, daughter of Henry VIII, was good to the people and good to the theatre which her people loved.

If you had been living in the time of Elizabeth I, you might have found things pretty lively. Englishmen like Sir Walter Raleigh and Sir Francis Drake were sailing to America and bringing back riches and romantic tales. There was a tingle of excitement in the English air. Teenagers, especially, felt that tingle. Something new was in the wind. Few knew just what it was, but it was a time of great expectations.

One lively thing was the theatre. You could see a new play every few days by such playwrights as Ben Jonson, Kit Marlowe, Will Shakespeare, and the popular writing team, Beaumont and Fletcher. You could see comedies and tragedies at the Globe, or the Fortune, or a place called just The Theatre.

You could see plays at school, too. You could be in them if you were talented and interested. School plays in Shakespeare's time? Yes, indeed, and some were presented in court at the invitation of the Queen.

Boys who were really talented sometimes got jobs acting with one of the professional companies. Some of them performed with a young actor named Will Shakespeare, and some performed in plays written by that same actor.

Being a young father himself, William Shakespeare liked working with boys. Some of his finest roles were written for boys. He must have been very lonesome for his own son and two daughters, who were at home in Stratford miles from the theatres of London. He must have been especially lonely after the death of his son. No doubt he poured his anguished heart into the parts he wrote for boys after that.

In his later years, Shakespeare was a member of London's most favored theatre company, known as The King's Men. That company was under the sponsorship of no less a person than King James the First, who succeeded Elizabeth after her death in 1603. If you could have tagged along with The King's Men for a few years, you might have waved goodbye to Will Shakespeare when he retired from the theatre around 1611 and turned his face toward Stratford and home. If you had been there to wave him off, you would have seen a light go out in the theatre of England, a light the likes of which would not shine again in England or the world.

Drama came as a fitting climax to the Renaissance. While it was hitting its peak in England, it was thriving in Spain and beginning to thrive in France. Spain had her playwrights, Calderón, and that prolific fellow, Lope de Vega, who wrote some 300 plays. France had Racine and Corneille, who emulated the classical tragedies of Greece. Because of this, their style is called *neoclassicism*. However, the man of the age, whose name ranks with that of Shakespeare, was the famous Molière (1622–1673), whose comedies still delight audiences all over the world.

Jean-Baptiste Poquelin, whose pseudonym was Molière, began as an amateur, with an amateur troupe. From an early age the theatre was in his blood but like many another actor he found it hard to make a living at acting. He learned the tricks of the commedia dell'arte players, who were plentiful in France and Italy in those days. Those traveling players of earlier times were still carrying on.

Commedia dell'arte refers to a kind of entertainment

that consists of improvised dialogue on a traditional plot. In these improvisations the players played stock characters and each actor was permanently assigned to his role. One actor might spend his life playing the villain. Another might spend his life playing the clown. The commedia dell'arte plots were all designed for a standard set of stock characters. These stock characters actually date back to the early Roman comedies. The commedia dell'arte was popular in Molière's time, and it is still popular today. It is, when it is well done, a fascinating kind of theatre.

The influence of the commedia dell'arte was evidenced in the first plays that Molière wrote, but there were things about the France of Louis XIV that he wanted to satirize, so he developed his own inimitable style. Nevertheless, the characters of his plays are prototypes, and they pop up in play after play. There is an old scalawag called Sganarelle, for example, in several of his plays. And there are always the young lovers, the impertinent maid, the faithful confidante, etc.

It is interesting that Molière began as an amateur. Let us never be ashamed of that word *amateur*. Most professionals are amateurs before they are professionals. That is as true in the theatre as it is in sports. Yet some critics treat amateurs with utter disdain. Perhaps that is because they do not stop to think what the word *amateur* really means.

An amateur is one who performs for the sheer joy of performing. A professional is one who performs for pay. Unfortunately the term *amateur* is sometimes applied to a performance that is bad. However, an amateur can strive for high standards and often achieve them, whereas a professional, though he is supposed always to be good, can be careless and do a performance that is worse than the work of some amateurs.

Molière was an amateur who cared deeply about his

work. He loved to act and his love was contagious. He gathered an acting group together and went about the provinces of France presenting plays, most of which he wrote himself. His little company went from village to village performing for nothing or for whatever they could get by passing the hat.

The Molière troupe had rough times, but things got better and better, and, after seven years of their vagabond travels, Molière and his fellow actors had a chance to appear before Louis the Sixteenth, King of France. It was a chance of a lifetime. Molière knew that if he pleased the King, his vagabond days were over. He and everyone in his company were as jittery as any ball team just before a championship game. Would they make it? Or would they flop? They flopped. The first play they did was terrible. Then Molière, his heart in his throat, begged to be allowed to do one of his own comedies. That one clicked. The King was enthralled and Molière and his group were launched on a professional career that led to long-lasting fame. Today the name of Molière is almost as great as that of Shakespeare, and his witty, satirical comedies are still favorites among both professional and amateur acting groups. His plays, all comedies, include *Tartuffe, The Misanthrope, The Imaginary Invalid, The Doctor In Spite of Himself, A School for Husbands, A School for Wives,* and *The Miser.*

Meanwhile, back in England, the theatre was in trouble. Soon after the death of Shakespeare in 1616 and of Ben Jonson in 1637, all theatres were closed. The trouble really began the century before. When Martin Luther started the Protestant Reformation in 1517, many of the Protestants went to extremes with their protesting and discarded everything that hinted of Roman Catholicism. That included drama. In England, that group of Protestants known as the Puritans did away with the King and set up a Commonwealth government under the leadership of

Oliver Cromwell and closed all of the theatres in England.

Drama died hard, however. In fact, it never really died. When the rule of England was restored to the royalty in the person of Charles II in 1660, drama bounced back. King Charles, a very fun-loving monarch, ordered the restoration of the theatres, and the restoration comedies began to flourish.

With the restoration came a new kind of theatre, quite different from that of the Globe and Fortune, where the Elizabethan actors had performed. The proscenium, or picture-frame, stage which had become popular in Italy now came to England. With the picture-frame stage came pictures in the nature of painted drops and wings. Scenery, which had not been used in Shakespeare's time, was now a vital part of every production.

Unlike the Elizabethan's theatre, where audiences from all walks of life were welcome, the gay, risqué, and brilliantly satirical comedies of the Restoration were strictly for the upper-crust society. The follies and foibles of that society were the subjects of the plays. The plays were comedies of manners, which means that the manners and customs of the upper classes were spoofed and ridiculed.

Some of the witty, brilliant men who wrote the Restoration comedies were William Congreve (1670–1729); William Wycherley (1640–1715); George Farquhar (1678–1707); Richard Sheridan (1751–1816); and Oliver Goldsmith (1728–1774). Although they came a century later, Sheridan and Goldsmith belong to this list because their plays were in the Restoration style.

Some of the best known Restoration comedies are *The Way of the World* (Congreve); *The Country Wife* (Wycherley); *The Beaux' Strategem* (Farquhar); *She Stoops to Conquer* (Goldsmith); and *The Rivals* (Sheridan).

With our discussion of seventeenth-century drama, we are in the final scene of the Renaissance. When did it end? For that matter, when did it begin? Historians may have definite dates, but as far as drama is concerned the Renaissance faded in and faded out. We use the word *faded* advisedly, because the transition was more of a fade-out than a blackout. Remnants of the Renaissance remained, and the theatre and the world are the richer for those remnants.

Some of those remnants became far-flung banners. Banners of French and Spanish culture flew in the fresh winds of the New World. French explorers were doing more than looking for Ponce de Leon's Fountain of Youth and Spanish Conquistadors did not spend all their time plundering the Aztecs. The French brought plays to their frontier Canadian settlements, and at the very time Shakespeare was in his prime in the early 1600s, Spaniards were giving daily performances in Mexico City.

About the time the Restoration comedies were getting underway in England, the first play was being presented in England's New World colony of Virginia. Virginia was friendly to drama. So was her neighbor, the colony of Carolina. It was in these colonies that the American theatre took early root. That was owing, no doubt, to the fact that the religion of these colonies was the Church of England. Henry VIII, who had divorced the English church from Rome when the Pope refused to recognize his divorce from his Queen, Catharine of Aragon, had never had any prudish opposition to the theatre. Prudish opposition to the drama was felt, however, by the English Puritans who settled along the coast of New England, and William Penn's Quakers who settled Pennsylvania. It was not until 1792 that a play was presented in Boston, and then it had to be advertised not as a play but as a moral lecture. As Americans, we are all indebted to the Puritans for many things, but the advancement of drama is not one of them.

Drama did advance in some of our American colonies, however. As early as 1752, nearly twenty-five years before

the American Revolution, an actor-manager named Lewis
Hallam brought a company of fifteen players from England
and opened in Williamsburg, Virginia, with a performance
of Shakespeare's *The Merchant of Venice*. The Hallam
players continued for many years, presenting the plays of
Shakespeare and other English playwrights in many colo-
nial settlements. Later the company produced a few
American plays. It had to be a few, because there weren't
many. The first one they did was called *The Prince of
Parthia* by Thomas Godfrey. That was in 1667. This, like
other early American plays, was an imitation of the English
dramas. It was not until 1787 that a purely American play
was produced. That was *The Contrast,* by Royall Tyler
(1757–1826). To Tyler goes the credit for the first American comedy.

There were other American playwrights who came along
during the years that followed the Revolution. One of
them was Washington Irving (1783–1859), the well-known
New York author, who wrote a play with Howard Payne.
Other names worth remembering are Steele MacKaye
(1842–1894) and George Henry Boker (1824–1890). Mac-
Kaye's *Hazel Kirke* set a box-office record for the New
World with 406 consecutive performances. William Dunlap (1766–1839) should be mentioned because of his
tragedy, *André*. This play had special significance because
its hero was a British officer who was tried and executed
by the American Revolutionaries. Dunlap gave his hero
a sympathetic treatment, but in spite of that fact the play
was popularly received by the American audiences at a
time when there was still strong feeling against the Tories
and the armies of King George III. The war had been
over only 15 years when the play was produced.

Dunlap should be remembered also because he was one
of the outstanding producers of that period and was author
of a history of the American theatre which was published
in 1832. He can rightfully be considered one of the

founding fathers of the American theatre. However, the theatre of America still had its moorings in the Old World, so let us return to the Continent and explore what was going on in Europe during the eighteenth and nineteenth centuries.

In England an architect named Inigo Jones (1573–1652), who designed the famous St. Paul's of London, was lending his genius to the proscenium stage and designing scenery the likes of which had not been seen before. Producers such as David Garrick (1717–1779) were taking full advantage of the picture-frame stage as they rehearsed their actors to make the most of their scenic possibilities. In Germany, Johann Wolfgang Goethe (1749–1832) was staging his famous *Faust* and other plays with stunning effect and, like Garrick and other directors of that time, was taking increasing pains with the training of his actors. With more artistic scenery came more artistic acting. Rigorous rehearsal schedules were introduced, and special attention was given to the minor roles.

A trend was underway to bring about a fusion of the theatre arts. The trend came to a climax with the appearance in Germany of the Meininger players under the leadership of George Saxe-Meiningen (1826–1914). He was a duke, with money, time, and big ideas. One of his ideas, his best, took form in his production of Shakespearean plays. Prior to this time, producers had rewritten Shakespeare to suit the acting star. Meiningen was faithful to the play and did not believe in stars. To him, every actor in his company was important. Much of his rehearsal time was spent with crowd scenes and the minor characters. He wanted all his actors to play together like a team of champions. He got what he wanted, and his troupe became the most famous company in Europe.

The Meininger spent eight years in preparation, studying, rehearsing, and perfecting their performances. Then they took Europe by storm. They had that long-awaited fusion of the arts. They brought new artistic standards to Europe, Russia, England, and America. It would be fair to say that the Meininger players were the main act of the nineteenth century. In Norway, a stage manager by the name of Henrik Ibsen (1828–1906) was influenced by the Meininger and quit his job to become one of the greatest playwrights of the century. In fact, the name of Ibsen ranks high among the dramatists of all time. With Ibsen came realism and plays of social significance. He shocked the world with his *Doll's House, Ghosts,* and *Hedda Gabler.* The shock came, because the expected happy ending never came. He saw the need for social reform and wrote about that need with the skill of a master craftsman. It is to the credit of his native Norway that his plays eventually caused social change in that state and in other nations.

Another prominent figure in the theatre who was inspired by the Duke of Meiningen and his players was the renowned Russian, Constantin Stanislavski (1863–1938). This son of a wealthy merchant was dabbling in amateur theatricals when the Meininger came to town. He was so enthralled by their performances that he was like a small boy at a circus. Now there was no longer any question in his mind. The theatre was to be his life. It was his life, and the impact of his life on the theatre of the world cast a long shadow across even men like Meiningen.

Who has not heard of "The Method?" Every stage-struck kid has heard the phrase, and many know it means the Stanislavski method. Among theatre students, the mention of "The Method" is usually the cue for argument. Although few people know what the method really is, most think they know, and want to air their views. They may be for it or against it, but whichever side they are on they are likely to be vehement, because "The Method" is always good for lively controversy.

However, there is much more to Constantin Stanislavski than "The Method." His acting method was only one of his contributions to Russia and the world. We remember him chiefly as the founder of the Moscow Art Theatre. Actually, he was a co-founder with a man named V. I. Nemirovitch-Danchenko (1858–1936). One of the most famous institutions in the world, the Moscow Art Theatre was more than a building. It was a school of theatre arts and a permanent acting company. It was a school with a new philosophy and an acting company with a new vision. The philosophy brought depth psychology to the art of acting, and the vision brought truth and excellence to the production.

Stanislavski went a step beyond Ibsen and brought naturalism to the theatre. In naturalism, the actors appear to behave on stage as they would behave in a life situation. Notice we say "appear to behave"—even in naturalism drama is bigger than life. However, in naturalism it is as though we were peeking through a window observing the people on the stage, who are presumably unaware of our observation.

There was a Russian doctor named Anton Chekhov (1860–1904). He wrote short stories to take his mind off the daily sufferings that he was obliged to witness. Stanislavski and Danchenko encouraged Chekhov to write plays. He did, and his plays were some of the greatest ever produced by the Moscow Art Theatre. In fact, they are among the great plays of the world's literature. The new Moscow Art Theatre opened with Chekhov's play *The Sea Gull,* and because of that, a sea gull became the theatre's insignia.

Chekhov's sense of humor, his compassion for humanity, and his prophetic perspective on the twilight of Czarist Russia gave his plays a special power and poetic beauty. His four best plays, *The Cherry Orchard, Uncle Vanya,*

The Sea Gull, and *The Three Sisters,* are still popular and are frequently performed in Europe, England, and America, as well as in Russia.

Another exponent of naturalism was the French director André P. Antoine (1858–1943), who was a contemporary of Stanislavski, his career starting in the late nineteenth century and extending into the early part of the twentieth. The young clerk Antoine spent his spare time acting in amateur productions, but he was soon bitten by the bug and resolved to spend all of his time in the theatre. He soon discovered he was a rebel with a cause. His cause was to reform the acting in the French theatre. Most professional actors in France were products of the Comédie Française, and so were trained in the classical tradition of acting. Antoine thought this kind of acting stilted and artificial.

Antoine formed a group of his own and began presenting plays in what he called his "Théâtre Libre." His performances attracted immediate attention. It was refreshing to hear actors converse instead of declaim. It was refreshing, too, to see plays that didn't always have happy endings. His naturalistic productions were often referred to as "a slice of life." The influence of Antoine, like that of Stanislavski, has stretched on into the twentieth century.

By way of contrast to the naturalistic theatre, we should look briefly at the work of the German producer, Max Reinhardt (1873–1932). To Reinhardt, drama was no slice of life. It was something that should be presented in a theatre with all the theatricality that the director, the actors, the artists, and the artisans could produce. Reinhardt loved huge, spectacular productions, and he staged them with matchless showmanship. He was a stickler for detail and rehearsed with a staff of stage managers who meticulously wrote down every direction he gave, in what Reinhardt called his *regie-buch* (production book).

These are but a few of the theatre titans who helped to bring the theatre into the twentieth century. Hundreds more could be mentioned. We will mention some, as we return to America for a look at the theatre in our own country.

When the American pioneers were conquering the wilderness and pushing ever westward, some attention to a native culture was beginning to bear fruit. Here and there artists, poets, and authors were beginning to emerge. In the theatre, however, culture came late. But what the theatre lacked in culture it made up for in commercial success. Perhaps it was that very commercialism that retarded cultural growth. In the theatre, the public usually gets what the public wants. Playwrights, producers, and actors as well, may strive to lift the public taste, and their striving will usually reap some reward, but if they are too far ahead of public taste their box office will suffer. Nevertheless, if we are to study theatre, we must face things as they are and as they were through the nineteenth century.

Near the middle of that century, in 1845, Anna Cora Mowatt (1819–1870) wrote a play called *Fashion*. It was well titled, because it set a new fashion in American comedy. It was not great literature, but it was good theatre, and it is a play that enjoys frequent revivals. Another feminine writer of that period was Harriet Beecher Stowe (1811–1896), a name made famous by her *Uncle Tom's Cabin*. It was an anti-slavery book which George Aiken turned into a play, and it became one of the greatest hits in the history of the American stage. It was first produced in 1852, a little over ten years before Abraham Lincoln ended slavery in the United States with his Emancipation Proclamation. In cities and towns, in hamlets, in great theatres, schoolhouses, and tent shows, *Uncle Tom's Cabin* was a perennial for many years. It has been presented as everything from a serious propaganda play to a sentimental comedy and from a musical extravaganza to a burlesque show. Topsy, Eva, and Uncle Tom, the most memorable characters in the play, became household names. It is the Uncle Tom of *Uncle Tom's Cabin* that people are referring to today when they call a black man who has sold out to the Whites an "Uncle Tom." Again, this play was not great literature, but it was colossal theatre. At least, it was colossal in the nineteenth century, when people were more sentimentally inclined.

There was an Irish actor who knew how to cash in on that sentimentality. His name was Dion Boucicault (1822–1890). He came to America in 1853 and soon became a successful actor-manager who also wrote plays. He was quick to sense the American taste and had a flair for adapting French and German plays to please that taste. Some of his original plays had Irish settings, but his most famous play, *The Octoroon*, dealt with a situation which was typically American even then—the race problem.

Augustin Daly (1838–1899) was one of the first to show concern for literary value in American drama. It is true that his own plays can lay small claim to literary merit. They were mostly melodramas and adaptations. Nevertheless, he encouraged other playwrights to strive for quality. His record as a theatre manager is distinctive.

James A. Herne (1839–1901) is another actor who turned playwright. After experiencing considerable commercial success, he deliberately turned his back on commercialism when he wrote a play called *Margaret Fleming*. In this play he tried earnestly to say something significant about the double standard. After writing such hits as *Shore Acres* and *Hearts of Oak*, he proved his serious concern for higher dramatic standards.

Bronson Howard (1842–1908) was another serious-minded playwright. Believing America could have plays comparable to those of Ibsen, he applied his fine mind and artistic integrity to the serious business of playwriting. The result was *Shenandoah*, which is generally considered the best play of the century on the subject of the

Civil War. Both he and Herne were striving for truth through art.

Around 1887 a young college graduate named Clyde Fitch (1865–1909) began to apply his college training to playwriting. Could a college man succeed in the theatre? Up until then there hadn't been many who had tried. By the turn of the century, Fitch had proved that it could be done, and done brilliantly. By 1901 he had four Broadway hits playing simultaneously. People began calling him the "Dean of American playwrights." It was a title he bore with a keen sense of responsibility. His plays, which were a little too obviously contrived, were far short of those of Ibsen and Chekhov, but they did boost the American standard a little.

Out of the youthful days of growing San Francisco, when the state of California was still young, came an Irish youth with a special gleam in his eye. He was David Belasco, and the gleam was the spark of genius. His love of drama came early and it led him to New York, where he became one of the most colorful of director-producers.

Belasco was famous for his realistic productions. He went to unheard-of lengths to achieve realism. He imported furniture from Japan for a Japanese setting, and went so far as to insist on having an original Beethoven musical score in a music cabinet which was merely referred to by a character in the play.

At a time when stage lighting was still in its infancy, he was an innovator of amazing lighting effects. With his stage electricians he would experiment for days until he achieved a sunset that was convincing. He was one of the first to do away with the flat lighting of foots and borders in favor of the subtle effects of spotlights. In his production of *Peter Grimm* the kindly ghost of old Peter Grimm appeared and vanished by means of spotlights.

Often referred to as the "high priest of Broadway," Belasco seemed to cast a spell over his actors. He had charisma, and by coaxing, scolding, throwing tantrums, and mesmerizing his actors, he was able to get what he wanted from them. He created stars, but they were his stars and rarely lived up to stardom for other directors. He was esteemed and feared, loved and hated; he was held by some to be a charlatan, and by many to be a rare genius.

Towering above Belasco and all the other producers and playwrights of the early part of this century is the name of Eugene O'Neill (1888–1953). With O'Neill, the American drama came of age. His plays were not only exciting theatre, but also great literature.

O'Neill, son of an actor, studied playwriting at Harvard under Professor George Pierce Baker. He was one of the first of many successful playwrights to study with the famous professor, who later moved to Yale to found the renowned Yale School of Drama.

O'Neill rose to fame in the early twenties, but his genius continues to stretch across the century. Although he died in 1953, he is still more frequently produced than many of his brilliant contemporaries, who include playwrights such as Maxwell Anderson (1889–1959), Robert Sherwood (1896–1955), George Kelly (1887–   ), Clifford Odets (1906–1963), Lillian Hellman (1907–   ), Arthur Miller (1915–   ), Tennessee Williams (1911–   ), and, more recently, Edward Albee (1928–   ), Marc Connelly (1890–   ), George Abbott (1887–   ), Moss Hart (1904–1961), Robert Anderson (1917–   ), William Gibson (1914–   ), William Inge (1913–   ), and Neil Simon (1927–   ).

America is indebted today to its producers, playwrights, and actors, but it is also indebted to dedicated groups determined to lift the standard of drama in this country. Three of those groups began as amateur organizations in 1915. They were the Neighborhood Playhouse, the Provincetown Players, and the Washington Square Players. Performing in small theatres, none of which seated much more than 300, these organizations dared to produce the works of new American playwrights, and their daring launched a new era on the American stage.

Even the briefest theatre history would be far from complete without some mention of America's unique gift to the theatre world. That gift was the musical. The roots of the musical reach back to the operettas and comic operas of the Old World. America can justly boast of being a world champion in the musical theatre. Aside from grand opera, in which Italy, France, and Germany excel, no country in the world can match our musical productions. Yet our prowess in this field is lately won. Furthermore, we are indebted to the operettas and comic operas of the Old World for the roots of our musicals. Those roots began to grow in earnest during the first quarter of this century. That was a period in which the musical comedy developed into a reputable art form.

Some of the memorable musical comedies of that period include *The Red Mill; Babes in Toyland; Blossom Time; Floradora;* and *The Student Prince.*

It was that king of jazz, George Gershwin, who first raised the curtain on the real American musical. The year was 1935 and the musical was *Porgy and Bess,* presented by an all-Negro cast. The story was serious, and both it and the music were pure Americana. Then, thanks to that remarkable team, Richard Rodgers and Oscar Hammerstein, the American musical soared into world-wide distinction during the decade of the forties, with such productions as *Oklahoma, Carousel, South Pacific, Brigadoon, Lady in the Dark, Carmen Jones, Finian's Rainbow,* and *Annie Get Your Gun.*

In the fifties, the great team was rivaled by another unforgettable combination, Alan Lerner and Frederick Loewe, who made theatre history with their *My Fair Lady,* which broke all previous box office records. Other musicals of the fifties include *The King and I, Guys and Dolls,*

Paint Your Wagon, Bells Are Ringing, Camelot, Gypsy, Li'l Abner, and *The Sound of Music*. In 1957 the earlier milestone, *Porgy and Bess*, was matched, if not surpassed, by another serious musical entitled *West Side Story*, with the musical score composed by none other than that idol of young people, Leonard Bernstein. In *West Side Story*, based on Shakespeare's *Romeo and Juliet*, the young toughs of New York's West Side met in rumbles with the young Puerto Ricans, and another typically American story was vigorously reenacted in vibrant dance, soaring song, and gutsy dialogue.

Many Broadway hits have been turned into musicals along with such incredible material as Cervantes's early seventeenth-century novel *Don Quixote* (*Man of La Mancha*) and Sholom Aleichem's Hebrew folk tales in *Fiddler on the Roof*. Tom Jones and Harvey Schmidt, from the University of Texas, turned French playwright Rostand's *The Romancers* into *The Fantasticks*, which continues a run that is indeed fantastic. Another bright, enterprising talent from Princeton, Clark Gesner, took the popular "Peanuts" cartoons of Charles Schultz and turned them into *You're a Good Man Charlie Brown*, which is one of the phenomena of the sixties.

These and hundreds of other musical productions on the American stage during the past twenty-five years have made musical theatre of sufficient importance to encourage performance of musicals in thousands of schools and colleges throughout the United States. The fact that some institutions now offer special training in musical theatre indicates the significance of the American musical.

5

This is Why It Goes On and On

Thus far, this outline has focused chiefly on playwrights and producers. Now let us concentrate on the actors and actresses as we present them in a kind of Who's Who.

A man's world is what the theatre seems to be. Only men acted in the theatres of ancient Greece and Rome. Only men acted in the theatre of Shakespeare's time. Most of the playwrights and directors have been men. Men have dominated the pages of this outline thus far. Are there no women in the theatre? Yes, and it seems only fair to begin our Who's Who with a discussion of the great women players.

Let us begin with the great Sarah. We could begin with any one of more than a thousand whose names deck the theatrical hall of fame. Even when we say "the great Sarah" we have to decide which great Sarah. There were at least two. One was Sarah Kemble Siddons (1755–1831), the other Sarah Bernhardt (1844–1923). Sarah Siddons came first historically, so let us take her first.

Sarah Kemble Siddons was born of a theatrical family. Both her parents and grandparents were actors. She began acting as a child and at the age of eighteen she married an actor in her father's company by the name of William Siddons. Early in her career she played Portia in Shakespeare's *The Merchant of Venice,* and apparently played it very badly. At least she was told that she was not very good. This was a tragic blow. Acting was her life. How could she live if she couldn't act? She did live, and she went on acting. She played any part she could get in any company in any part of England. She spent the next six years trouping about the provinces playing a great variety of roles. All the while, she was developing technique and style. She discovered the power of concentration and developed remarkable control of her body, voice, and mind. When she returned to London, she was an immediate triumph at the age of twenty-seven. Her stunning career continued until her death in 1831. It was a career made possible by her intelligence, her industry, and her determination to succeed.

Sarah Bernhardt came later. She came out of France to mesmerize the civilized world. She too suffered humiliating discouragement as a young actress. She, like Sarah Siddons, won out by work and will. She had an ego that drove her like a fiend. She loved the glamour of the stage, and made herself a glamourous part of it. It is said that her voice was like a musical instrument, and she played it with the artistry of a virtuoso. Every role she did was powerfully and beautifully executed. Every role she did was larger than life. She seemed to have a kind of divine dominion over her audiences, and it was no small wonder that she was able to tour America with a guarantee of 100 performances in four months at a fee of $1000 per performance, plus 50 percent of all receipts over $4000. Her love of glamour was not limited to the stage. She traveled in a private railway car equipped with parlor, bedroom, dining room, and kitchen. The incredible Madame Bernhardt went on enthralling audiences with a long career which everyone thought would surely end, and end tragically, when, at the age of 75 she had to have one of her legs amputated. Even that did not stop her. She went on acting until her death at the age of 79.

Eleanora Duse (1859–1924), that mystery queen of the stage from Italy, was also enthralling audiences during the career of Sarah Bernhardt. We call her "queen" because she ruled the stage and ruled the hearts of men and women who packed the theatres to see her. We call her "mystery queen" because the nature of her power is still a secret. Some say her beauty was her genius. Some say it was her voice. Some say it was the way she spoke and moved that made her magical on the stages of the world. Apparently she had a kind of Joan Baez simplicity, and like that popular folk singer of the sixties, she was a star with a special luster. She seemed to have a way of gathering up her very soul and pouring the whole of it into a role. She was not the intellectual actress that Sarah Siddons was, and did not have Bernhardt's concern for glamour, and yet she willed her mind and heart into each part she played, making it as pure as poetry.

Another little lady of remarkable stature was England's Ellen Terry (1847–1928). She, like Sarah Siddons, was a daughter of actor parents, and like both Sarahs began acting at an early age. At the age of eight she performed with her father and sister in over 100 performances of Shakespeare's *Winter's Tale*. She was born in the middle of the nineteenth century, and long before that century was ended, when she was only twenty-seven, she had interpreted more than 75 different characters. She won the hearts of playgoers wherever she appeared. One of those hearts was in the breast of a drama critic named George Bernard Shaw (1856–1950), the same G.B.S. who later became one of Britain's most distinguished playwrights. Shaw and Miss Terry carried on a lively correspondence throughout the heyday of her career. This was an honor Ellen Terry would later share with another British actress whose intimate correspondence with the great G.B.S. was even more notorious.

That British actress was Beatrice Stella Campbell, who graced the British and American stages for more than half a century. She made her entrance into the world in 1865 and died in 1940. She filled that span with regal action, playing many of the great roles and winning favor on her tours of America as well as in her native England. She was the one and only actress Shaw felt he had to have to play Eliza Doolittle in his famous *Pygmalion,* a comedy that became even more famous as the musical *My Fair Lady.* Although she engaged in such realistic bits of stage business as blowing her nose in the midst of a highly emotional scene, her acting was more theatrical than realistic. She had a great sense of style, and a kind of magnetism. Instead of reaching out to her audience she seemed to pull her audience up to her. It was a cozy arrangement that compensated for her British reserve.

In contrast to the theatrical acting of Mrs. Patrick Campbell was the psychological approach of Russia's Alla Nazimova. Born in St. Petersburg (Leningrad) in 1879, her timing was perfect to enable her to take advantage of the new naturalism fostered by Stanislavski. Her concern for character motivation also made her right for the women of Ibsen's plays. She played the great Ibsen roles with depth and power and seemed to perform everything she did with new insight. She brought to the United States in the early part of the twentieth century a fresh approach to acting. Until then, most American actors had emulated the British and, to some extent, the French. From Madame Nazimova, American actors caught a glimpse of the Stanislavski Method.

Let us not suppose that America had no great actresses of her own. She did. There were Lillian Russell (1861–1922), Fay Templeton (1865–1939), Blanche Bates (1873–1941), and Minnie Maddern Fiske (1865–1932). There were Ada Rehan (1860–1916), famous for her Katharine in *The Taming of the Shrew;* petite Maude Adams (1872–1953), immortalized in her *Peter Pan;* Margaret Anglin (1876–1958), celebrated leading lady in producer Charles Frohman's company; and Maxine Elliott (1868–1940), whose name extended beyond her distinguished acting career when, in 1908, she built the theatre which bears her name. Later came Helen Hayes and Katharine Cornell, Lynn Fontanne and Eva Le Gallienne, who formed her own repertory company in the late twenties. The list could go on and on, this list of women in the theatre, but there are gentlemen to consider, and we must spend some space on them.

Selection is a frustrating business. No matter if we are selecting actors or actresses, some of the great ones are certain to be left out. Where, then, to begin? that is the question.

We might begin with track star John Raitt, who after graduating from college became one of America's foremost actor-singers. Or, we might begin with Cleander, that second actor added by Sophocles back there in ancient Greece, or with Richard Burbage, of Shakespeare's time. To start at either extreme, ancient or contemporary, would involve us with far too many names, so let us make an arbitrary start by returning to David Garrick, mentioned earlier, who lived from 1717 to 1779. In a time when actors had a tendency to play each new role like all the other roles they played, David Garrick was a rebel. He rebelled against playing every role like every other role he had done, and took great pains to make each role distinctive. When he played the ancient mad King Lear, for instance, he studied madmen and aged people. He tried to copy nature, and therein lay the key to his success. He felt there was too much bombast and oratory in the acting of his day, so made a great thing of moving and speaking as people do in life. He, and the players who worked with him, held as their goal the interpretation of drama in the likeness of life itself.

One of the English actors guilty of bombast and oratory was Sarah Siddons's younger brother, John Philip Kemble, who lived from 1757 to 1823. His acting was apparently what people would call today "elocution." The term is usually derogatory. In this kind of acting, the manner in which the words are spoken becomes more important than the words themselves. The actor is working for a striking effect instead of an honest expression. John Philip did have a following, and it was fashionable to be among his followers, but we mention him here chiefly to point out the kind of acting that Garrick was against.

Another rebel against the Kemble kind of acting was a harum-scarum kind of misfit named Edmund Kean (1787–1833). At least he began as a harum-scarum misfit. Nobody knows for sure, but it is thought that he was born in 1787. Nobody knows for sure, because he was born out of wedlock, but that was only one of his many handicaps. He was undersized, underweight, and under almost every conceivable disadvantage. He was the neighborhood nobody whom everybody considered most unlikely to succeed. He was an uneducated waif with a raspy voice and incredible cockiness, and an incredible lack of education, yet this waif had presence. He had a talent for reciting and a talent for charming. He charmed his way into a troupe of strolling players by the time he was sixteen years old. Furthermore, he continued charming his way up the rickety ladder to fame, and by the time he was 25 he was the leading actor in a company at Dorchester. He carried on Garrick's rebellion against artificiality and brought a thoroughly personal touch to every role he played. His approach to famous Shakespearean roles was entirely original, and no one could actually anticipate how he would interpret a role. His interpretation of Shylock in Shakespeare's *The Merchant of Venice,* for example, was so packed with insight and lightning-like flashes of truth that the audience applauded practically everything he did. In direct contrast to the pedantic, meticulous Philip Kemble, Edmund Kean was definitely and unashamedly an emotional actor.

If you could have watched a rehearsal in the early years of the nineteenth century, you might have been amazed at the indifference of the actors, especially the stars. You would have found them walking through their parts unemotionally, saying their lines with no expression. They were like some inexperienced actors today who have the naïve notion that an actor doesn't need to play a role for its emotional value until he is playing it for an audience. Only an amateur thinks he can perform without adequate rehearsal. That is what professionals believe today, and it's what an old pro named William Macready believed in the early 1800s. He was a professional in the best sense of the word. He worked hard in the profession. He learned industry from his father, and that industry landed him an acting job at the age of seventeen. He was not so handsome as an actor likes to be, and he had a rather dyspeptic disposition, but he was smart enough to overcome these handicaps, and he knew the importance of proper preparation. He made the most of every rehearsal, feeling his way into the character, and experimenting freely with the values of each scene. He had a theory that the harder he worked at rehearsal the more relaxed he was likely to be in performance. The theory worked for him, and it worked for those actors who were wise enough to profit from his precept and example. Unlike Kean, he was not an inspired genius, but what he lacked in talent he made up for in practice. It is amazing what industry and desire can accomplish. Macready's career is a good example.

Another example is the career of Henry Irving (1838–1905). We should say "Sir Henry Irving." In England, great actors are sometimes knighted. Sir Henry was one of the first to be so honored. He was a long way from that honor when he was a struggling young actor in the middle of the nineteenth century. He was another youngster who had more points against him than he could count. He was awkward, he had poor speech, and he looked like anything but an actor. The point was, he wanted to be an actor. He wanted it badly enough to enroll in an acting class in London. It was a hard course, and he worked hard. He snatched eagerly at any part he could get, and acted two years with an amateur group. Finally he had a chance to go professional trouping the provinces. Then came his debut in London. It was a dismal flop. A man with less determination would have stopped there. He didn't. Undaunted, he went back to the provinces. He spent the next seven years playing the provinces, playing such cities as Liverpool, Manchester, Birmingham, Dublin, and Glasgow. In those seven years he acted 180 different roles. Finally his diligence began to pay off. When the American actor Edwin Booth came to England, Irving had a chance to appear in several Shakespearean productions with the great American star. After seventeen years of diligent study and hard experience, Henry Irving himself became a star, and eventually manager of his own company, a company in which no less a leading lady than Ellen Terry acted.

Edwin Booth (1833–1893) had a special place in history and in the very heart of America. He is special not only because he was the greatest American actor of the nineteenth century, but also because he had the extreme bad luck of having an infamous brother. His brother was John Wilkes Booth. He was also an actor. We might say he was a very bad actor. At least one of his off-stage acts was unpardonably bad. But his entrance for this act comes later. Our hero is Edwin, not John Wilkes. Edwin Booth made his New York debut at the age of seventeen in 1850, right in the middle of the nineteenth century. He had begun acting professionally only a year before, yet in 1851 he played the title role in Shakespeare's *Richard III.* He then went west to play in San Francisco and the mining towns of California. Wherever he went, he found fame, and his fame grew and spread. In 1864 he was back in New York for a gala performance of Shakespeare's *Julius Caesar,* in which he played Brutus and his brother John Wilkes played Marc Antony. The very next night he opened in the title role of Shakespeare's *Hamlet.* It was a record hit, playing 100 performances. Meanwhile, the War Between the States was coming to a close. General Robert E. Lee surrendered the Confederate Army at Appomattox on April 9, 1865. Five days later, on Good Friday, President Lincoln and his wife went to see Miss Laura Kean in a comedy called *Our American Cousin* in the old Ford Theatre. John Wilkes Booth was not in the cast. However, he made an unexpected entrance which cannot be forgotten. After firing the shot that ended the life of Abraham Lincoln, John Wilkes Booth leaped from the Lincoln box onto the stage, disrupting the action, as he hobbled to his escape through the wings with a broken leg. Shocked, horrified, and grieved, Edwin Booth retired from acting. Later, he burned every prop and costume that had belonged to his brother. Fortunately, Edwin Booth came out of retirement in the winter of 1866, to appear once more in his favorite role, Hamlet. He was fearful. How would he be received? As the brother of an assassin, would he ever again be accepted? The answer came in the ovation he received. The cheers and applause were like a thunder storm. His acquittal was clear and definite. Edwin Booth bowed low and wept.

Coquelin is a funny-sounding name. Coquelin was a funny man, but a man with serious ideas. He was a French actor born in 1841, and he talked and wrote a good deal about the art of acting. He believed that an actor was putty in his own hands. He believed that an actor molded himself as he would mold wet clay to fit the nature of the role he was to play. He wrote a book entitled *The Actor as Artist*. He believed that the actor as artist need not actually experience the emotion he is portraying, but rather he must convince the audience that he is experiencing this. He likened the actor to a pianist who does not need to feel the emotional content of the music he is playing. True to the classical French tradition, Coquelin advocated the mastery of technique. It is through vocal and pantomimic techniques that the actor moves his audience to laughter and to tears. One of the great actors of the century, Coquelin exemplified this theory in his own brilliant performances. He was a voice for his time, and a voice which still has validity.

It would no doubt redound to the glory of our heritage if we could tell of the success of Afro-American actors. For reasons known to us all, we cannot. Until recent years there were so few! There was a Negro company of players called the African Grove Players in the early part of the nineteenth century, doing well in New York, on Bleecker Street, until a gang of white hoodlums disgracefully put them out of business.

However, out of that group of players, one name lights up the Black horizon. It is the name of Ira Aldridge. He was in his early teens when he was with the African Grove Players, and he was determined to go on acting. He did, and he rose to great fame, though he never again appeared on an American stage. His fame was won in the cities of Europe, where he was the toast of royalty. In Sweden he performed repeatedly at the special invitation of the king. The Tzar of Russia awarded him the Cross of Leopold, and from the King of Prussia he received the Order of Chevalier.

In Moscow, young Russian students were so enamored with the famous Black star that they unhitched the horses of his carriage and themselves pulled the vehicle through the streets, chanting his name. His popularity was such that even celebrities had to obtain tickets well in advance. Playgoers, young and old, were spellbound by his magnetic personality, his rich voice, and his native talent.

Aldridge was a versatile actor. He played a great variety of roles, many of them in the plays of Shakespeare. His greatest role was Othello in Shakespeare's play of that title. Another role for which he was famous was Mungo, the singing slave, in a little-known play called *Padlock*. His career spanned four decades before he died in 1867 at the age of sixty in Lodz, Poland.

Where did he come from, this man who was such a credit to his race and to the theatre of the world? Although he was born a half century before the Civil War, he was not a slave. His parents had long since been freed. His father was a Presbyterian preacher, and a man of considerable histrionic talent himself. Being a preacher, he had misgivings about his son's entering the theatrical profession, so sent him to Scotland for schooling, but young Ira found his way to London and into the role of Othello before he was twenty. Like many a wise father before and since, the elder Aldridge stood by his son once he accepted the fact that Ira had to follow his own calling.

Where did he come from, this Black actor who could not follow his calling in his own land? Some say from New York, some say Maryland. Those who hold to the latter maintain that he was born in Bel Air, Maryland, the same town where Edwin Booth was born. Regardless of his birthplace, he is immortalized in a memorial in the Shakespeare Memorial Theatre at Stratford-on-Avon, and that is a distinction few American actors have achieved.

The Black theatre picture has brightened considerably in recent times. Out of the Civil Rights movement and the desegregation legislation of the past two decades has come the rise of Black power, which, in its truest sense, merely means the awakening of Americans, black and white, to the awareness of human rights. Black culture, being a part of our heritage, is finding expression in the theatre, as is evidenced by the recent establishment of the Negro Ensemble Company of New York. Under the direction of Robert Hooks and Douglas Turner Ward, it is recognized as one of the leading repertory organizations.

Nowadays many Black actors are adding their significant talents to the American stage. Let us identify a few, not by way of singling them out from other talents who might be equally worthy of mention, but rather to illustrate the importance of the Black impact on our theatre today.

James Earl Jones brightened the Broadway scene when he opened in *The Great White Hope* in 1968. In the role of the pugilist Jack Jefferson, he won standing ovations night after night.

The late Lorraine Hansberry, in her highly successful play, *A Raisin in the Sun,* provided opportunity for several Black actors to add to their professional stature, among them Sidney Poitier, Claudia McNeil, Diana Sands, Ruby Dee, and Glynn Truman, and Beah Richards, who understudied Miss McNeil and later played the role in Los Angeles.

Now hailed as one of our most popular actors, Sidney Poitier wanted to learn to act so badly that he studied acting at night while pushing a handcart in Manhattan's garment district by day in order to make a living and pay for his acting lessons. Having a limited education and being told he was fit for nothing but manual labor, he had to triumph over discouragement time after time. When he first auditioned for the Negro Theatre in New York, he was turned down and told to forget any idea he had about a career in the theatre. Though his pride was wounded, he refused to be downed, and came back for another try and was accepted, landing a part in an all-Black production of *Lysistrata.* It was thirteen years before he got his first real break in *A Raisin in the Sun.*

Ruby Dee is married to Ossie Davis, one of the most

frequently employed Negro performers during the past two decades. Diana Sands was a winner of many awards, including the Off Broadway Magazine award, for her performance in *The Egg and I;* the Outer Circle Critics award for best supporting actress in *A Raisin in the Sun;* the International Artist award for her film role in the same play; and the Theatre World award for her performance in *Tiger, Tiger.*

Diahann Carroll, in the musical *No Strings,* written for her by Richard Rodgers, glorified the American Negro woman as she had never been glorified before. In the role of a sophisticated fashion model, Miss Carroll brought rare enrichment to Black feminism. She was given the Antoinette Perry (Tony) award in 1962 and the *Cue* Entertainer of the Year award in 1961.

Roscoe Lee Browne came to the theatre from a teaching position. How do such things happen? Always a lover of plays, he simply made up his mind one evening that he was going to act. The next day he auditioned for Shakespeare's *Julius Caesar,* which was being cast for a New York summer production. He was cast immediately as the Soothsayer and, thanks to his native talent and well-trained voice and body, has been doing minor and major roles ever since in various American theatres. He is currently associated with the Center Theatre Group at the Mark Taper Forum in Los Angeles, where he spends much of his time visiting schools and colleges reading plays and poetry for spellbound young audiences.

No rostrum of Negro players would be even partially complete without mention of that grand lady of song and stage, Ethel Waters. Her birth and her career coincide with the twentieth century. Born in 1900, she began at an early age as a cabaret singer and landed her first Broadway acting assignment in 1927 in a play called *Africana.* Then followed many musicals, including the unforgettable *As Thousands Cheer.*

Her first nonsinging role was Hagar in *Mamba's Daughters* when she was thirty-nine. However, the straight role for which she is probably best known is Berenice Sadie Brown in *The Member of the Wedding*, the role of a cook in which she blended riotous humor with sorrowful understanding. Always, Miss Waters sings and plays her way straight into the hearts of her listeners, just as she wrote her way into many hearts in her autobiography, *His Eye Is On the Sparrow*. A tribute to her professional status is the fact that she was a member of the Executive Council of Actors Equity and Vice President of the Negro Guild of America as far back as the early forties.

Claudia McNeil, who also played Berenice in *The Member of the Wedding*, and, as mentioned before, was in the original cast of *A Raisin in the Sun*, was asked some years ago by an aspiring young Negro actress if she thought it worthwhile for a Black to attempt a career in the theatre. The answer lies in the swelling triumph of Black theatrical art throughout America. It is obviously worthwhile for those who have talent and perseverance. Success is never achieved without struggle, but it seems clear that the American theatre is increasingly color blind.

This Who's Who among actors has been very sketchy. It has to be, in a brief outline like this. In fact, this outline itself is sketchy. We are simply touching some of the peaks in theatre history. There are many other peaks well worth exploring, to say nothing of the valleys. So far, we have limited our discussion to the theatre of the Western world —Europe and America. What about the East? What about the Orient? Certainly, the theatre of the non-Western cultures is too fascinating and too important to neglect entirely. Therefore, let us at least touch base for a brief Oriental orientation.

Like the nations of the West, India, Japan, and China have enjoyed theatre for centuries. As was the case in Greece and Egypt, drama began, at least in India and

Japan, long before the Christian era. It began as a religious ritual and developed into a sophisticated art. In India, scholars wrote about the art as early as the second century A.D. In China, there were schools for actors long before Shakespeare's time. In Japan, an actor named Zeami wrote many books about the art of acting more than a hundred years before the theatre renaissance in England.

The theatre of the Orient is quite different from the theatre of the West. In the West, the theatre has moved in the direction of realism. In the East, it has taken the route of symbolism. Western drama imitates life by holding the mirror up to nature. Eastern drama presents the essence of life through established conventions. The visual convention consists of costumes, masks, gestures, and dance-like movement. The movement is somewhat like our Western ballet in that each movement and each position of the body has a conventional and traditional meaning. The vocal conventions are established through a skillful use of the voice in what sounds to us like artificial voice patterns. The vocal patterns are sometimes spoken, sometimes chanted, and sometimes sung quite melodically. The voices are frequently accompanied by flutes, drums, and stringed instruments. The total effect is a little like our opera and ballet, though to our Western eyes and ears it seems even more artificial.

The property man is a unique characteristic of the Chinese theatre. Dressed in black, he is presumably invisible. When not needed, he sits at one side of the stage casually drinking tea or reading a newspaper. When an actor needs a prop, he is there on the stage, placing the prop in the actor's hand precisely on cue. If a prince must kneel, the prop man places a pillow for his knee. If Lady Precious Stream wants tea, the prop man hands her a cup of tea. If a great general is off to the wars, the prop man hands him his sword, and may escort him, holding up a sign that says "10,000 troops."

A kind of kissing cousin to the Chinese property man is the Japanese puppeteer. The puppet theatre, with its life-size dolls, is one of the oldest institutions in Japan. The dolls, which are themselves great works of art, are operated by highly skilled men dressed in black. These are the celebrated puppeteers. It takes three puppeteers to operate a single doll. Each puppeteer must train from childhood. Each hopes to become one day a master puppeteer, a highly esteemed position.

In addition to the puppet plays, most of which are very old and have great literary merit, there are two other kinds of Japanese drama, Nōh and Kabuki. The Nōh play is very ancient, is religious in its nature, and is primarily for the aristocracy. Then there is the Kabuki play. It is more recently developed and has a more popular appeal. Usually, five Nōh plays make up an evening's entertainment. It would be more correct to say a day's entertainment, because in Japan, as elsewhere in the Orient, a theatrical event may last from 11:00 A.M. until nearly midnight. In the Kabuki theatre, a platform called "the flower walk" (Hanamichi) runs from the rear of the auditorium along the left side of the audience to the stage. The actors make their initial approach to the stage along this walk. It is also used for marches and processions within the play.

Attendance at the theatre is an important social occasion. Often an entire family will attend in a group. People go to see and be seen as well as to enjoy the play. The interval between the plays is a time for visiting and eating. Rice cakes and teas and other Oriental goodies are everywhere in evidence.

If you lived in the Orient and wanted to be an actor, you would already have lost several years of training. In China and in Japan, boys ambitious for an acting career often start their training at the age of seven. We say "boys" because the Oriental theatre, for the most part, engages only male actors. It is a man's world. One exception is

Japan's Takarazuka all-girl revue, composed of four hundred singing and dancing young actresses who are all models of Japanese decorum and highly disciplined artistry. In India, too, women have, at times, been members of the acting companies. However, acting in the Orient is a rough and vigorous profession, and training for it is hard work. An actor must have the body of an athlete and the voice of an operatic singer. For this he must train, and train hard, for years.

It is interesting to imagine what might have happened if the East and the West had not gone their separate ways. If the drama of the Orient and the drama of the Occident could have developed together through the centuries, we might have had a many-splendored theatre. We might also have had a better understanding among the peoples of the earth. It may be that that understanding and the many-splendored theatre may still lie within the realm of possibility. Japan in recent years has welcomed Western drama, and we in turn are growing in appreciation of the Oriental theatre. There is a mingling of cultures. Out of that mingling may come respect and understanding. When we can respect the drama and the art of other nations and when they can respect our art and drama, our mutual fears may one day be replaced by mutual friendship. It may be that the evolution of the theatre can serve that end. It may be that you and your generation already have the vision of that prospect and that the finest chapter in history will be created by what you do.

6

This is What To Do

If you want to act, this chapter is for you. It's not a magic formula that will turn you into a star overnight. Usually, stars that appear overnight never last long. Even those in the sky lose their luster in the light of day. There is no short, easy road to stardom. There is a road, and we may help to put you on it, but for the time being stardom is just something to dream about. For the time being we are interested in what you can do to make yourself a better actor.

We assume that you have learned your theatre ABC's. If not, go back and learn them. Turn back to the chapter entitled "This is the Theatre" and be sure you know, and know thoroughly, all those rudimentary stage techniques. When you know up from down, right from left, how to cross, how to turn, how to sit, how to stand, then you are ready to learn what to do next.

An actor prepares. That statement is so obviously true that Stanislavski wrote a book about it. All along the way an actor prepares. The first stage of preparation is a thorough grasp of the ABC's. The next stage of preparation might be called stage presence.

Stage presence takes the place of stage fright. Some people seem to have been born with stage presence; others have to develop it. There is a kind of presence that cannot be acquired, but that is not the kind we are talking about. We are talking about the kind of self-confidence that comes when you know your way about the stage and feel at home there. Stage fright is nothing but the absence of that kind of confidence.

When we talk of stage fright, we are not thinking of that hollow feeling in the stomach that comes just before curtain time or just before you make your entrance. That is a perfectly normal, healthy feeling, and the best of actors never lose it. In fact, old troupers often say if they don't get that feeling, or something similar, they are likely not to give a good performance. That feeling should never be confused with real stage fright. Stage fright is a fear of failure, so let us have an honest look at failure.

In the theatre, failure is part of the process of learning. Rehearsals are filled with failures. We have to fail in order to succeed. Success is achieved through a series of failures. We fail, so we try again; we fail, we try again, and each time we do a little better. We may not know we are doing better, but the odds are a hundred to one that we are. Progress is merely a series of corrected mistakes. If we are afraid to fail, we are afraid to progress. So let's have done with the bugaboo of failure. Everyone in the theatre should feel free to fail, free to make mistakes, free to fall flat on his face, because that is precisely what everybody is doing all through the rehearsal period.

Stage fright is really a self-conscious conceit. Or perhaps we should say "subconscious" or "unconscious" conceit. The person who suffers from stage fright is usually not aware of the fact that he is conceited. In fact it may come as quite a surprise to discover that he is. But what are you, if not conceited, when you imagine that you are above failure? Who are you, that you shouldn't fail? Are you superhuman? What's so special about you? Everyone else in the cast is going to fluff and flub and appear quite stupid from time to time. Why shouldn't you? Relax. Be human. There is no disgrace in falling short as long as you keep trying. Learn to take things in your stride, and you will soon stride with confidence.

Once we accept failure for what it is, a guidepost toward success, we are well on our way to conquering stage fright. The rest of the way is to be found in rehearsals. The object of rehearsals is preparation. When we are prepared, and know we are prepared, we are not afraid. We may have a tingle of excitement, and a few anxious moments, but when we are really prepared, we are secure. With security and self-confidence as rewards, it should be easy to take rehearsals seriously, very seriously. With security and self-confidence as rewards, there is great incentive in preparing for rehearsals. The more we study our lines, the more we practice our roles, away from rehearsals, the more confidence we are likely to have in rehearsals, the fewer mistakes we are likely to make. The fewer mistakes we make in rehearsals, the more we build up our confidence for performances.

There is a third step for building up self-confidence and overcoming fear. It, too, has to do with preparation. Suppose you are one of those individuals who are naturally tense or naturally shy or naturally nervous. There is a prescription that is good for all three of these ailments. It might be convenient if the prescription were a pill, but it isn't. Pills are risky things to take before a performance. About the only safe kind is vitamin pills. Our prescription can be explained in two words. Those words are *breathe* and *relax*. Breathe and relax! It sounds quite simple. It is. Try the following exercises, and you will discover how simple it is.

1. Pant like a tired dog on a hot summer day. Keep your mouth open and breathe in and out very rapidly. Place your hands at the base of the ribs with your fingertips across your abdomen. Notice the slight movement

at the base of the ribs and the definite rapid movement of the diaphragm. The diaphragm is the big muscle that goes around your torso at the base of your ribs. Pant as long as you can without getting dizzy. If you get dizzy quickly, it means only that you should pant more often.

2. Pant again, and this time laugh as you pant. With a ha ha ha and a ho ho ho work up a good, lusty laugh. Girls, don't giggle. Giggling does no good. Laugh! You will find this exercise much more fun if several of you do it together. You may find yourself getting a little hysterical but try to keep enough control to stay with the exercise. Remember, the idea is to laugh and to pant. What you are actually doing is making a sound on each exhalation. If you are doing it properly, you are taking in a quick breath between each "ha" or each "ho." Naturally, this is not an exercise to do on the stage when the audience is gathering. Usually there is some place back stage where at least this much vocalizing can be carried on without disturbing anyone. Incidentally, this is an excellent limbering-up exercise for each rehearsal.

3. Lie on your back and laugh. Place a heavy book or a comparable weight on your solar plexus and bounce it up and down as you laugh. This will toughen up your diaphragm, and an actor, like an athlete, needs a good firm diaphragm. Your diaphragm should be so firm that you could take a good punch in the solar plexus and not have it faze you. Add that to your goals if your diaphragm is soft and flabby.

4. Still flat on your back, force all the air out of your lungs. Do this slowly, then slowly inhale, taking all of the air your lungs can possibly hold. When you think you have all the air you can possibly take in, try taking in a little more. Then slowly exhale, forcing all of the air out of your lungs, and when you think it's all out, try to whistle. You probably won't whistle, but you will discover you can still exhale a little more. Repeat this exercise

three or four times, and after you have been practicing the exercise for a few days, try repeating it from six to ten times. This is a great exercise for developing lung capacity and breath control.

5. In a standing position, with your fists clenched and held above your head, take in a big breath and tense every muscle in your body. Then suddenly exhale and relax, letting your body slump and your arms fall to your sides. Next, try going into the tense position very slowly, slowly taking a big breath, then slumping and exhaling very slowly. Repeat the latter several times.

Any or all of these exercises will help dispel jitters or tensions, and should do a lot to help overcome shyness. Who can be shy in the midst of a lot of laughing panters? However, there is still another cure for shyness. It is projection.

Usually, a shy person is afraid of the sound of his or her own voice. We are not talking about that normal shyness of which all of us have a touch. We mean the mousy type of shyness. How do we help that timid soul who is afraid to speak above a whisper?

If the timid soul has participated in the "ha ha ha" and the "ho ho ho" mentioned above, he or she is already on the way to a solution of the problem. The first step is to discover that there's a connection between the voice and the lungs. A faint voice simply means a lack of breath support. Therefore, Miss Shy and Mr. Timid, on stage please!

Now, Miss Shy, take a big breath and say "Ouch!" Mr. Timid, you take a big breath and say "Ouch!" Neither of you is "ouching" loud enough. Miss Shy, suppose you pinch Mr. Timid, and Mr. Timid, suppose you pull the hair of Miss Shy. Thank you, that makes your ouches a little more convincing, but they're still not loud enough. However, they're improving, so let's take the next step.

The next step is to have Miss Shy remain on stage and

Mr. Timid go to the rear of the auditorium, and from those positions carry on a conversation. Being shy and timid, they will be awkward at first, but with a little patient encouragement, they will begin to ask each other questions. Suddenly they will find themselves projecting, because they will have to project in order to communicate. Communication has furnished motivation for projection. So, having found voices that they didn't know they had, and having discovered that they can project their voices, Miss Shy and Mr. Timid now have new motivation for speaking up and speaking out.

What is that new motivation? The sound of their own voices. Voice is an important part of personality. People know you by your voice. As you expand your voice, you expand your personality. As you expand your personality you expand your world. Your world becomes wider because there is more of you to fill it. As an actor you want to fill it. As an actor, your immediate world is the theatre, and you want to fill it. You want to fill the stage with the sound of you as well as the sight of you. Even if you're playing a character who is shy, you must project that shyness to the back row of the house.

As an actor, one of the things you do is develop personality. You do that by putting the best of yourself into everything you do. The best of yourself is almost always better than you think it is. An actor must believe in himself. He must believe also that he can become a better self. He does this by acting. He acts as though he were what he would like to be. If he knows he is too shy, or too retiring, he deliberately acts like an extrovert. If he knows he is too aggressive, he deliberately acts with more reserve. Gradually he becomes the kind of person he wants to be.

If you are a lonely person, you are not alone. You have lots of company. Most people are lonely, especially people your age. Loneliness can be good for your acting. It makes you more sensitive to your role. It also makes you more appreciative of the other people in the cast. Remember, they may be lonely too. Together you develop a camaraderie that overcomes loneliness. As you work together in a play you develop friendships.

Friendships are good for self-esteem. Good friendships with good people develop self-respect. An actor needs self-esteem and self-respect. They build self-confidence and self-reliance.

In drama we learn to give and take. Friendships are built on the capacity to give and take. We give our friendship and accept the friendship of others. In this give and take we learn how important it is to like ourselves. Others won't care much about us if we don't like ourselves. Yet the more we like others the more we are likely to like ourselves. This liking and being liked is part of the give and take in drama.

You like yourself best when you are at your best. You are at your best when you know what to do and do it. You already know part of what to do. We have just been discussing it. There is more, of course, and in order to discuss it, let us assume that you have just been given a good part in a good play. This is what you do.

You thank your director and let everybody know how grateful you are. Then you read the play. You have read it before, of course. You probably read it at least once or twice before you went to the tryouts. Now you read it with a new interest and a new zest. Now you read with the idea of getting the whole play thoroughly in mind. Notice, we say "the whole play." It would be a great mistake for you to read only your part and ignore the rest of the play. You must know the play before you can possibly know your part.

When you feel you know the play thoroughly, you are ready to begin studying your role. You read your lines and think about them. You read them aloud. You try to make your voice express the lines intelligently. You read for feeling as well as for understanding. You will quickly discover that you cannot read for feeling or understanding without reference to what is said in your presence when you are on stage. Therefore, the studying of your role means the careful reading of everything that everybody else says in the scenes you are in.

Acting is as much reacting as acting. As you read the lines of others, think how you will react. Often, how you react is more important than what you say. Certainly, if you don't react, what you say will not have much importance. Your familiarity with the lines of the other actors will prepare you to listen intelligently when you hear those lines in rehearsal. On the stage there are moments when listening is more important than speaking. If you have done your homework on your role, you will be ready to make the most of those moments.

Be sure to take a good sharp pencil or two with you to rehearsal and be prepared to write in your play script all the directions your director gives you. You may imagine you can remember the directions without writing them down. Don't take a chance. Valuable rehearsal time is too often wasted by actors who fail to write their business in their scripts. When the rehearsal is over, go through the business the director has given you, saying your lines as you do so, and trying to match the business to the lines. Try to find the reason for every movement the director has given you. Often the director will tell you why you are to cross from one area to another, but an actor should be prepared to figure out his own justification or motivation for everything he does.

Usually the memorization of lines is not called for until the director has completely blocked the play and the actors have had an opportunity to become thoroughly familiar with their roles. Memorization comes hard for some and more easily for others. One thing is certain, nobody can memorize lines without working at it. Nevertheless, we have a trick or two to give you that will speed up your memorization and make the process easier. First, ask yourself whether you memorize best with your eyes or with your ears? If you are the kind that sees the words in your mind's eye, you will probably do best by simply reading the script over line by line and fixing the words in your visual sense. If you are the kind who memorizes best by hearing the sound of the words, then you should speak the lines aloud when you are memorizing them. However, even if you memorize visually, you will put yourself ahead of the game if you also say the words as you are reading them. By this process you are using both your visual and your oral memory senses. Furthermore, by saying the lines aloud, you may be eliminating diction problems that are likely to give you trouble later on.

There is another trick to memorizing that is extremely helpful. If you happen to have keen spatial and tactile senses, this third way may prove to be the best of all for you. The trick is for you to walk through your stage business while you are reading and saying the lines. By this process you are matching words and movement and also establishing your position in relation to the other actors. This method has an added advantage. You are memorizing your business as you are memorizing your lines. Some actors combine all three methods. They are the smart ones who usually are the first ones to have their lines cold.

You will discover, if you have not already made that discovery, that you can have your lines cold in your room and forget them when you get on stage. This is a universal problem, and should be no source of embarrassment to you. You should simply stumble through as best you can and not hesitate to call "line please" to your prompter when you're stuck.

Of course, you should know your lines perfectly as soon as possible. The sooner you know them, the sooner you will be able to get down to the serious business of putting the finishing touches on your role. The finishing stage is usually the most exciting time in the rehearsal period. It is then that you can begin to give dimension to your character. All along you have been thinking a good deal about what your character looks like, how he walks, how he talks, what kind of clothes he wears and how he wears them, and how he conducts himself in general. In this connection, we have some guidelines to suggest.

In the role you are playing ask yourself the following questions:

1. How old am I?
2. Am I rich, or poor, or moderately well off?
3. How well educated am I?
4. What is my position in my family?
5. What is my family like?
6. Where do I live?
7. How well do I get along with people?
8. Am I happy at what I am doing?
9. Am I an extrovert or an introvert?
10. Am I aggressive or retiring?
11. How ambitious am I?
12. What is my relation to the other characters in the play?
13. Which ones do I like; which ones do I dislike?
14. What is my goal in the play?
15. What is my objective in each scene?
16. How do I go about trying to get what I want?
17. Am I subtle, or forthright?
18. Am I gentle, or demanding?
19. Where am I when I am not on stage?
20. Where have I come from when I make an entrance?
21. Where am I going when I make an exit?
22. What is my mental and emotional state before I make an entrance?

23. What will it be when I've made my exit?
24. Am I in familiar surroundings when I'm on stage? Or is the environment strange to me?
25. Do I stride, waddle, shuffle—how do I walk?
26. Do I slouch, or hold myself erect—how do I sit?
27. How do I stand?
28. Do I lead with my chin, or my head, or my chest, or stomach, or feet?
29. Do I occupy a lot of space, or am I the kind of person who tries to make himself small?
30. What are my characteristic gestures?
31. If I were an animal, what might I be? A dog, a cat, a bear, a chicken, or what?
32. What do I sound like? Am I big-voiced, or soft-spoken?
33. Am I elegant or crude?
34. Am I talkative, or am I inclined to talk very little?
35. Is my voice resonant, or is it nasal or guttural?
36. Do I speak with a dialect, or is my speech fairly normal?

You may not be able to apply all of these questions to the part you are playing. On the other hand, these questions may stimulate other questions. In any event, some such catechism will help you bring more than a superficial understanding to your role. Such questions also point up the fact that acting is a good deal more than walking on the stage and saying lines. However, the saying of the lines is also very important. The lines are the actor's verbal connection with the audience. They are his sole channel of oral communication. This means they must be spoken with understanding, and it is not enough for the actor to understand them. He must convey his understanding to the audience. Before the audience can understand the meaning of the words, it must be able to understand what the actor is saying. It can only do this when the actor is projecting and pronouncing his words distinctly.

We have talked about projection earlier in this chapter. Now let us talk about articulation. It is not enough for dear old Aunt Cora, sitting in the back row, to hear the voices of the actors. Aunt Cora wants to know what they are talking about. She wants to hear their words. Aunt Cora isn't fussy about the diction. She doesn't want the actors all to sound like Oxford graduates. She just doesn't want to sit through an evening of garbled speech. Let us remember that audiences are made up of Aunt Coras, Uncle Oscars, and all their sons, daughters, brothers and their sisters and their cousins and their aunts. They have all come together with one thing in mind—to enjoy the play. They can't enjoy it if they don't know what the actors are saying.

We are leading up to a discussion of diction. In fact, we are up to it. But why discuss it? Everybody knows that diction has to do with the way words are pronounced and articulated. Everybody knows that every young actor needs help in this area. So why don't we do something about it? We will. Or better still, you will. We will furnish the diction drills, and you will practice them. Then when you've learned to pronounce your vowels clearly and articulate your consonants distinctly, you and Aunt Cora will both be elated.

Let us begin with vowels. Most people don't pronounce them with enough fullness of tone. Furthermore, many people don't make a sharp enough distinction between the vowels. How many people do you know, for instance, who pronounce "pen" like "pin" or "just" like "jist"?

In the following combinations of words appear all of the vowels that are most commonly used in the English language. Say these words aloud, and listen carefully to your pronunciation of the vowels. Each word contains a different vowel sound. Can you hear a difference?

1. You could know daughter from father.
2. See Bill get there and fight.
3. Up above bird.

Do not be surprised if your ear does not hear much difference in the way you pronounce the vowels in "up above bird." Likewise, you may hear little difference between the vowel in the word "get" and the vowel in the word "there." Also, you may not detect much difference between the vowel in "daughter" and the vowel in "from." Nevertheless, there is a difference, and in time you should be able to hear it.

When two vowels are combined, the result is a diphthong. Many people turn vowels into diphthongs. They shouldn't, of course. Diphthongs, too, are often mispronounced. The three that are most likely to give trouble are found in the following words: day, night, hour. Have you ever heard someone say "dye-ay" when he means "day?" Or say "noight" when he means "night"? Or say "are" when he means "our"?

Practice saying the various vowels and diphthongs and listen carefully to the sounds you are making. With practice you can surely improve the sound of your vowels. You can improve each vowel sound, too, by sustaining it. The beauty of our language lies largely in its vowels. If you think of the vowel as a singing tone, that will help. In fact, singing itself will help. When you are singing, you have to sustain the vowels in order to produce the singing tone. It goes without saying that singing is good for the speaking voice. Every actor should have at least a few singing lessons.

Here are a few drills that should help you improve the sound of your vowels and diphthongs:

(Speak each sentence slowly, making the vowels clear and well sustained.)

1. There is doom in the gloom of the Dooms-Day Blues.
2. What hood would do good if he could?
3. Go throw your robes to the roaring Romans.
4. Daughter oughter wash with water.
5. Anon the dawn dawns on the lawn.
6. Farms and fodder bother father.
7. Seeing scenery in the sea is but seeing weeds to me.
8. Rick can lick both Nick and Mick and still spill Bill.
9. I'll bet my pet your pet gets wet.
10. Don't tear your hair with rare despair! The bears are there and everywhere.
11. The bad fat cat fell flat and that was that.
12. We might be right, we might be bright, if not at night, at twilight.
13. Up, up, you pup, and lick my cuff.
14. I love that dove above the glove.
15. Hear how the brown hound howls to cow an owl.

In the above paragraph we have covered the vowels and diphthongs that are most commonly used. Now let us tackle the drills for consonants. These drills will be of little value unless the consonants are articulated sharply and clearly. In fact, it is advisable to exaggerate the articulation each time you practice the drills. When articulation of the consonants is exaggerated, the muscles of the tongue and lips become trained. Then they will do the job for you on stage without your having to think about it.

Repeat each of the following sentences four or five times. Be sure you sound the consonant at the end of the word as well as at the beginning and in the middle.

1. Bouncy baby Bobby bounces about on the brawny back of baby Bobby's big brother Bill.
2. Calmly, collectedly, cleverly, Clarence carried Carrie to the carriage.

3. Danny's Dad did deeds with Danny's dollars designed to double Danny's dollars.
4. Fighting friends of Frank and Fay are faithful friends of Fred and Faith.
5. Gus got Greco out of the ghetto but gave up getting the ghetto out of Greco.
6. Happy Hattie had a hat that hid her homely head, but happy Hattie hid her hat behind her homey bed.
7. Jim and Jane and jolly Toppy jogged along in Jim's jalopy.
8. Lucky Lem and little Lil live like lilies by the mill.
9. Mother's mini-minded Myrt mindfully mends her mini-skirt.
10. Nellie napping from noon to night never notices her plight.
11. Prim and proper Percy Pace puts people in their proper place.
12. A rambling wreck from Rambling Rapids rode roughly through the rambling rabbits.
13. Seven snozzly sisters smartly smocked surprised the seven civil servants whom they shocked.
14. Tommy told Terry and that was that. Then Terry told Tommy to tell twenty tattlers.
15. Very virtuous virgins value both song and verse, and very virtuous Virginia could have values that are worse.
16. We will welcome weary wanderers be they wealthy, wise, or poor.
17. Zany Zora got a zero in both Xylophone and zither.
18. Hither, thither, thence, and thither, Thelma's thimble is lost in thistles.
19. Surely Sherry Shelley shall shun short-shouldered shysters.
20. White whales whimpering when they die whisper "whither, whence, and why."

In that last sentence, pay particular attention to the "h" sound. Many people have the habit of dropping the "h" sound entirely in the words that begin with "wh." This is a result of carelessness. The "h" should be sounded. Other consonant sounds that seem to give many people trouble occur in those words beginning with "sh," "th," and "s." Very often the "sh" or the "th" will be substituted for "s." If you like to be technical, this is known as a lateral lisp. Practice saying "shy," "sigh," "thigh"; listen carefully to the difference between "s" and "sh," and "sh" and "th." Try not to substitute either "sh" or "th" for "s."

Meanwhile, as you work on these drills and try to improve your speech, you are growing in your role. There comes that exciting moment when you appear in costume for the first time and have all your scenery, properties, and lights. Once you are fitted in your costume, you will be smart to seize the first opportunity to get on stage and walk through all your business. For this, you may need special permission from your director, but it is something that is worth trying. It is hoped that you have had an opportunity to rehearse in front of a full-length mirror from time to time. Now it is time to return to that mirror in costume. Return to it again when you are in make-up. Work out with lines and pantomime before the mirror. What you see in the mirror will either give you confidence or cues for correction. In either case, it should be a part of your role-studying procedure.

Another part of role-study procedure should be tape recordings. Both audio and video tapings of rehearsals are highly beneficial. However, they can be beneficial only in ratio to the time and intensity with which they are auditioned and studied. Listen intently to the audio recordings of your voice and study thoroughly the video recordings of your movement and pantomime.

Finally, when all the drills and aids and rehearsals are

behind you, and the last notes from the last dress rehearsal have been read to you and the other members of the cast, the great moment is at hand. The night has come. The audience has assembled. The curtain rises, and the play begins. You have that moment of panic. Everyone has. You cover it, though, with calm control. You take a few deep breaths, run through your panting exercise, and remind yourself that you are prepared. So, the show is on, and you are on, and you know now what it is you do.

You know what to do, and you've learned a little about how to do it. At least, you've learned enough to know that there is still lots for you to learn. When you have learned, you have earned your right to work in the theatre. You have taken that all-important step across the threshold.

What could be a more fitting conclusion to this chapter on what to do than a self-evaluation? Here are a few questions designed for that very purpose.

1. Regardless of what others may have said about your performance, what did you think of it? What did you like? What did you dislike?

2. If you were doing the role again, what changes would you make? If you were going through the rehearsal period again, what would you do differently?

3. How would you rate your state of preparation— excellent, good, fair, poor?

4. Were you relaxed throughout the performance? If not, what might you have done to remedy the situation?

5. When you came on stage, did you merely make an entrance from the wings, or did you suggest that you were coming from wherever it was you were supposed to be before you entered?

6. When you were on stage did you find yourself worrying about lines, cues, and business? Or were you able to concentrate on your character and throw yourself into the reality of the situation?

7. How well did you listen? How well did you react?

8. Did you make the best possible use of hand props and items of costumes?

9. How would you rate your communication with the audience? Excellent, good, fair, poor?

10. If your communication was not what you hoped it would be, did you feel it was because of lack of projection, lack of articulation, or lack of interpretation?

11. Do you feel you made intelligent use of body positions? NOTE: if you stared at the actor with whom you were playing most of the time and kept yourself in profile, the answer is "No."

12. Did you make the best use of movement and pantomime? Did you feel that you were telling your story by what you did as well as by what you said?

13. How would you rate your cooperation with the other members of the cast—excellent, good, fair, poor?

14. Using the same scale, how would you rate your off-stage conduct?

15. On the basis of your experience, in what areas do you feel you need help?

These questions, along with others which they may stimulate, should help with your personal evaluation. Here are a few additional questions to help you discover what kind of acting you are doing.

1. Do you find yourself forcing the character? Forcing your voice? Or forcing facial expression? Do you feel yourself going out of control? Do you do things on the stage impetuously, things you have not rehearsed? Do not confuse this with spontaneity. You can play with spontaneity and still perform as you have rehearsed. In fact, if you can improvise your way out of a line jam, that is all to the good. However, if you add business or expressions, or even line readings, that you have not rehearsed, that is not so good. Nor is it good to force.

2. Had you seen some other actor do the role played? If so, did you find yourself trying to imitate that actor?

In any event, did you find yourself imitating some other actor or were you trying to create the role out of your own imagination? The imitation of other actors can be dangerous. A creative approach is always best.

3. In the playing of your role, were you able to throw off your own identity? Were you able to become the character so thoroughly that your friends forgot it was you playing the part? Or were you always yourself reading the lines and going through the business? Ideally, you should be able to subject your personality to the personality of the character you are playing.

4. Did you feel every emotion that you were attempting to project? If so, did you feel it throughout the performance? Or, on the other hand, did you experience the emotion at some time, or perhaps several times, during rehearsals, and then merely tried to represent what you had felt in performance? If your answer was yes to either of these questions, your performance probably was believable. The important thing to remember is that what you feel is of no consequence unless you can make the audience feel it.

Acting is believing, but it is also make-believe. What does the actor do? He makes the audience believe in the make-believe. All that we have said in this chapter can be summed up in that simple statement. The audience knows that what is taking place on the stage is not real. But the audience wants to pretend with the actors that the make-believe is real. That is the essence of drama and the enchantment of the theatre.

7

This is How To Do It

"Play ball! Swim—run—box—fence—learn karate—do anything to keep your muscle tone firm and your lungs active."
If you think that is advice to a ball club, you're wrong. It is advice to a group of student actors. The words are those of a professional director, and he was talking to student actors, both men and women. The advice was in response to the thing they all wanted to know: "How do we make it in the professional theatre."

How to do it—?? Keep healthy, strong, and physically active. Drama is no field for softies. The vigorous daily workout of the actors in the American Conservatory Theatre is evidence of that fact. Many of the A.C.T. actors are veritable acrobats and tumbling artists, and all of them are athletic. Obviously, one of the secrets of the "how to do" is to keep in excellent physical condition.

However, there is more to acting that keeping physically fit. There is more to it than all the skills we talked about in the last chapter. It is one thing to know what to do, and something else to know how to do it. So, how? The question persists. Nobody knows all the answers, but some of the experts know a lot of the answers. So, if we pool some of the answers of the experts, we may have a clue to the how. So let us now examine what some of the stars can give us regarding how they go about tackling the business of acting.

Begin with your feet. That's what the Broadway and television star James Daly does. When he is cast in a role, one of the first things he thinks about is what kind of shoes he is going to wear. If that sounds odd, give it a second thought. It may be that the character you are going to play wouldn't even wear shoes. If he wouldn't, that certainly tells you something about the character. If he would, the kind of shoes he would wear would also tell you something about the character. Shoes have a great deal to do with how you walk and stand, and how you walk and stand goes right back to the nature of your character. Of course, the star of *J.B., Period of Adjustment,* and many other Broadway hits, as well as the television series "Medical Center," does not stop with his feet and his shoes. You may be sure his heart and his mind get into the act.

An actress who also pays a lot of attention to her feet is Lynn Fontanne. She is very much concerned with the movement of her feet. She cannot feel right in a role until her footwork is right. N.B.C. producer Robert Hartung, in directing Miss Fontanne recently, was aware of her practicing one exit for more than an hour in order to get her footwork right. Lynn Fontanne and her husband Alfred Lunt are America's great acting team. Their brilliant, polished performances, in such productions as *The Taming of the Shrew, Idiot's Delight,* and *The Visit* have thrilled and delighted audiences for four generations. Mr. Lunt shares his wife's meticulous concern for technical perfection, and they are both inexhaustible rehearsers. It is more usual than uncommon for them to stay on and rehearse long after the other members of the cast have left the theatre.

Sidney Poitier, mentioned before, another star of stage, film, and television, tries to match his acting technique to personal experience, and vice versa. When he is rehearsing a role he is constantly searching his own background for emotional experiences that are similar to those of the character he is studying. He likes to fix the emotions of his character while he is in rehearsal so that he is free to live the part in performance. Poitier believes that talent is a gift that should be cared for and he believes that anyone with the gift can succeed regardless of the color of his skin. He has demonstrated his gift in plays such as *Lysistrata, Anna Lucasta,* and *Raisin in the Sun.*

Study voice—study dance. That is the advice that Shelley Winters would probably give you if you were to ask her about the how of acting. She feels that American actors in recent times have not had enough training in voice and body techniques. You no doubt know the play *The Diary of Anne Frank.* It was Shelley Winters who won an Oscar for starring in the movie of that play. She has a great respect for the stage and believes, as the Greeks did, that the theatre is a temple. She believes that many people go to the theatre for the same reason that they go to church, to receive spiritual inspiration.

Miss Winters's idea is worth pondering, because some of the things that are presented nowadays do not seem very spiritual. Nevertheless, her idea is a kind of ideal that is worth a second thought. It is one thing to learn how to succeed in the theatre, and it may be quite another thing to learn how to succeed without sacrificing your ideals. Miss Winters's credits include *The Country Girl, A View From the Bridge,* and *The Night of the Iguana.*

One actress who seems not to have sacrificed her ideals is that darling of the American stage and television, Helen Hayes. She has some pertinent advice to give. Her advice may sound more like the kind of advice you would get from your teachers instead of an actress. She advises young people to stay in school as long as possible. She feels that anyone going into acting should be as knowledgeable as possible and should have a great understanding of all kinds of people. The many diverse roles she has played in her long career suggest that she herself knows a few things about people. Some of her roles include *What Every Woman Knows, Victoria Regina, The Show-Off,* and *Harvey.*

Miss Hayes attaches great importance to technique, and her own technique is impeccable. However, she would be the first to tell you that technique is only a tool for interpreting character. The ability to portray character is the mark of true talent. That is her contention. She has another interesting view about talent. She believes that talent is nothing more nor less than the ability to understand the human heart. Helen Hayes has firsthand knowledge about the human heart. Her own heart was almost broken when she lost her teen-age daughter, who was a victim of polio. Furthermore, she is the widow of the late Broadway producer Charles MacArthur. It is no wonder that Miss Hayes prefers to appear in a play that has a message, and that she enjoys doing a role that will enable her to say something significant to her audience.

If you are the kind of an actor who likes to sit around for hours at a time analyzing the play and dissecting your role, you would probably not be very comfortable in the presence of Helen Hayes. She thinks that a little verbalizing may be all right, but a little is enough. She is one of those actors who like to get on the stage and go to work. In this respect, she is like the Lunts and like another great lady of the American stage, Katharine Cornell.

If you can imagine what it would be like to appear in a new play every week, you may get an image of Katharine Cornell's background. She learned to act by acting and she did her acting in a stock company. While she was performing nightly in one play she was rehearsing daily in another. This is how American actors learned their trade before the colleges and universities developed departments of drama. It was a school of hard knocks, and Katharine Cornell is one of those who graduated with honors. Her honors included such roles as *The Barretts of Wimpole Street, St. Joan,* and *Dear Liar.*

It should not surprise you to learn that Katharine Cornell believes there is no teacher like an audience. She would therefore probably admit that experience is the best teacher. However, it is her contention that imagination is even more important than experience. She would probably advise you to read extensively, to do a lot of dreaming, and to try your hand at creative writing and anything else that will develop your imagination. She would, of course, be the first to agree that the study of drama is one of the most effective ways of developing imagination.

It may be that Miss Cornell is right about imagination's being more important than experience. Or it may be that imagination is neither more nor less than the correlation of experiences. That is the opinion of a famous actor named Morris Carnovsky. He would urge you to recall your experience when you are studying a role. Experience, of course, might include the things you've dreamed or read about. But everything that has happened to you can be helpful. It is a matter of selecting and arranging the experiences of the past. You remember and select those experiences that seem to fit the character you are studying. Then you arrange those selected memories to fit the feelings of the character you are playing. Mr. Carnovsky leans heavily on what is called "inner technique." What do we mean by inner technique? That is something you have to have in order to remember experiences at will. It is the technique that enables you to feel and project what is called for at the very moment you need it. Mr. Carnovsky believes strongly that an actor should have inner technique, but he is just as enthusiastic about the importance of outer technique. In other words, he would advise you to train your voice and body, but he would also insist that you train your memory.

There is another reason for mentioning Morris Carnovsky. That reason goes beyond the fact that he has played such roles as *Uncle Vanya, King Lear,* and the male lead in *Tiger at the Gates.* However, the fact that he has played so many great roles does contribute to our main reason for mentioning him. Look for the humanity in the part you are to play. Look for the humanity in the people whom you know. Look for the humanity in everyone you meet. That is what he urges every young actor to do. In looking for humanity in others, we find it in ourselves. That is his point. That is our point, too, at least our main one, in mentioning Mr. Carnovsky.

Be liked. Be funny. Be honest. This is the kind of advice the late comedian Bert Lahr would have been most likely to have given you. Be liked. An actor must be liked by the audience. In fact, an actor hopes he will be loved by the audience. One way to win the love of the audience is to love the audience. If you can feel yourself sending out waves of loving good will to all those people out front, those people are pretty likely to send back waves of loving good will to you. However, in addition to loving the audience, you must be good. You must know what to do and how to do it, and you must do it well. Audiences admire expertness. Audiences love the artist who excels.

Be funny. That was what comedian Bert Lahr was. How about you? Are you funny in the comedy roles you play? Do you get laughs on your comedy lines? How did Bert Lahr do it? He said it is a matter of instinct and timing. We would add that intelligence goes along with instinct. You have to be intelligent enough to know what is funny, or intelligent enough to know what ought to be funny. In other words, you have to know when to expect a laugh. At what particular word in a line is an audience likely to laugh? At what particular moment in a sequence of stage business is the audience likely to laugh? These are intellectual decisions. Instinct can then assist you in the reading of the line or the executing of the business. Instinct may also help you to discover your own comedy technique. However, there are some basic comedy techniques which we will discuss later in this chapter. Timing is a part of that technique, so we will save it for later.

Be honest. Honesty is, of course, basic to all acting. It doesn't matter whether you are playing a comedy role or a serious role. The audience must feel that you are playing with honesty. Say the lines of the play as though you are thinking them for the first time. That is one way to be honest. Respond to your cues as though you were hearing them for the first time. That is another way to be honest. Act as though you mean what you say, and play every situation as though it were true to life. Practice at being honest on stage. It will help you to be honest in everyday life.

Anne Bancroft is an actress who certainly believes in honesty. In addition to her memorable role as Anne Sullivan in *The Miracle Worker,* she has appeared in such productions as *Two for the Seesaw* and *A Cry of Players.* She is convinced that the one thing an actor cannot afford to be is phony. Furthermore, she knows that an audience is quick to spot a phony. If you are supposed to laugh, you must laugh; if you are supposed to cry, you must cry. That is her simple credo, and she brooks no nonsense about it. Nevertheless, she plays with brains over heart. She believes that an actress should always be in control of what she is doing. Anne Bancroft is another one who doesn't waste much time discussing theories of acting. She likes simply to get on the stage and act. However, she wants to be prepared when she gets on the stage. This often means a great deal of background reading. She is never satisfied merely to read the play and learn her part. She may read as many as a dozen books to help her bring more background to her role. Background, she believes, helps her to free herself on stage. If there is anything Anne Bancroft is on stage, it is free. She is an actress who plays with great abandon. Yet, she is always in control of that abandon.

It must be clear by now that all actors do not solve in the same way the problem of how to act. There was Paul Muni, for instance, who held that the heart is more important than the brain. He went straight to the emotional life of his character and played his roles with his heart more than his head. This does not mean that he didn't use his head when he was on stage. He did, of course, but he believed that acting should not be bound by any specific style or method. Some of his outstanding productions included *Key Largo, Death of a Salesman,* and *Inherit the Wind.* One thing that should be passed along to you from Paul Muni's acting is his listening. He was a great listener. He listened intently to everything the other actor was saying. He said this helped to keep him fresh and alert in his role.

This head and heart controversy is a good subject for conversation. It is an argument you may want to carry on with your friends in drama. Whether you accept Mr. Muni's heart-over-head theory or prefer Miss Bancroft's head-over-heart approach, it is clear that both have something significant to contribute. An actor such as Paul Muni tended to lose himself in the role. Anne Bancroft, on the other hand, says that she does not lose herself. Instead, she likes to feel that she is finding herself. She feels that great living is more important than great acting, and through her performance she wants to give her audiences something that will make them want to live greater lives.

John Raitt has a similar attitude toward his acting. He, too, likes to feel that he is giving his audiences something to live for. He would like to feel that his performances help people to leave the theatre a little better than when they entered it. Even if he can reach only one person, he feels his performance has been worthwhile. In fact, he often performs as if he were playing to one person. He says there is almost always someone in the audience that he knows, some aunt or uncle, some distant cousin, or an old friend—and for that person it is an opening night—and Mr. Raitt makes it a gala première. John Raitt has a trick at auditioning that should be passed along to you. When he reads for a dramatic role, he goes about it in a way that is totally different from the standard procedure for try-outs. He looks at the script for a long time without saying a word. Then he lifts his eyes and says a line. He does not read it from the script. He says it. He then studies the next line, spending perhaps as much as a minute or more on it, then puts down the script and says the line. By this process he is able to use his eyes as well as his tongue to suggest what he can do with the role. It is a trick worth trying next time you read for a part. Mr. Raitt has starred in *Oklahoma!*, *Carousel*, and *The Pajama Game*.

Another John from another country has advice for you of a different nature. We refer to the British actor, Sir John Gielgud, who has been as popular in America as in England. Being a Britisher, he was, of course, trained in the English classical tradition. That tradition places great emphasis on voice and body training. That tradition also centers around the performing of Shakespearean roles and the standard Restoration comedies. Sir John thinks that American actors are inclined to spend too much of their time analyzing their characters. He thinks that we in America put too much emphasis on psychological motivation. He recommends more work in voice and diction. He advises actors to take up fencing and dancing in order to develop agile bodies. He says that actors need to learn how to stand still without fidgeting. He says they need to learn how to speak beautifully. It is a good thing to be reminded by Gielgud that there is beauty in the English language, and beauty in the spoken word. "Speak the speech, I pray you, as I pronounced it to you, trippingly on the tongue." That was Shakespeare's advice to actors. You may recognize it as the opening line in Hamlet's speech to the Players. Gielgud, too, would have you "speak the speech." He would have you speak it "trippingly on the tongue," which means speaking from the front of your mouth with clear, clean articulation. British actors are expected to be able to speak and move. If they can't, they simply don't act.

Sir Laurence Olivier puts it even more forcefully. He says that an actor should be so well trained that he carries out directions automatically. Sir Laurence can speak with considerable authority, because he is not only one of the greatest actors in the world, he is also an excellent director. Being highly disciplined himself, he expects and gets discipline from the actors who work under him. He wants his actors to be able to respond immediately to his direction, because in that way he can discover any mistakes that he has made. He thinks actors shouldn't waste time talking about abstractions. An actor gets the scene right by doing it over and over. Discussion is no substitute for rehearsing. That is his contention.

If you need additional information to help you identify and remember these two great British actors, here are some of the productions in which they have appeared. John Gielgud has appeared in *Hamlet, The Lady's Not for Burning,* and *The Three Sisters;* some of Sir Laurence Olivier's greatest successes were *Macbeth, Becket,* and *The Skin of Our Teeth.*

Speaking of Shakespeare, we should actually do more speaking of Shakespeare. In our schools there is too much reading of Shakespeare and not enough speaking of Shakespeare. When we say "speaking of Shakespeare," we don't mean merely talking about him. We mean speaking his lines. Read his plays aloud. That is the only sensible way to read them. If you get a chance to appear in a Shakespearean play, jump at it. It should be no more awkward to speak the poetry of Shakespeare than to sing a song. That is the opinion of Michael Langham, another Britisher. Mr. Langham was director of the Shakespearean festival at Stratford, Ontario, Canada, for several years. Shakespeare is a great challenge to young actors, even to very young actors. We must remember that Shakespeare wrote for young actors. In his time all the female roles in his plays were performed by boys. What boys could do in Shakespeare's time they could do today. How can they do it? They can't, if the only training and experience they have is in second-rate realistic comedies. Boys, and girls as well, can learn to play Shakespeare by playing Shakespeare. They may not sound like Sir Laurence Olivier or Sir John Gielgud, but nobody expects them to. Of course, the language of Shakespeare's plays is different from the everyday language of most people. However, the plays of Shakespeare are a magnificent part of our language heritage and we should steep ourselves in that heritage at the earliest possible age. Most of our great men and women during the past three or four centuries have been well-versed in Shakespeare. Abraham Lincoln, Sir Winston Churchill, Eleanor Roosevelt, and John F. Kennedy were all fond of quoting Shakespeare. Shakespeare is not for actors only. He is for people in all walks of life.

You may not feel that Shakespeare is your "thing," but give him a fling. You cannot be sure what your thing is until you have experimented with a lot of things. Many young people develop a prejudice against Shakespeare before they have given the Bard a fair chance. Teachers are sometimes at fault. Often they are asked to teach a class in Shakespeare without having adequate preparation. For this they can't be blamed entirely. They can be helped, however, by you. Your interest is their inspiration. Your enthusiasm can turn a dull class into an exciting adventure. If you are assigned a Shakespearean play to read, read it aloud. Then ask if several of you can read a scene aloud in class. Remember, Shakespeare wrote for the stage, not for the classroom. The sound of his poetry cannot be appreciated by merely reading his words silently.

We are stressing Shakespeare because the ability to speak his lines is a strong answer to the "how" we are in search of. How do young actors become good actors? Certainly, mastery of Shakespeare is one of the ways. This is so true that we want at this point to give you a recipe for acting that is guaranteed to make you a better actor.

The recipe is Hamlet's advice to the Players. Read it. Study it for meaning. Memorize it. Speak it aloud every day for several weeks. Then take the advice of young Hamlet. Do not "mouth your words" or "saw the air too much with your hands, thus." Here are the highlights of Hamlet's speech:

Speak the speech, I pray you, as I pronounced it to you, trippingly on the tongue. But if you mouth it, as many of our players do, I had as lief the town crier spoke my lines. Nor do not saw the air too much with your hand, thus, but use all gently, for in the very torrent, tempest, and (as I may say) whirlwind of your passion, you must acquire and beget a temperance that may give it smoothness. O, it offends me to the soul to hear a robustious periwig-pated fellow tear a passion to tatters, to very rags, to split the ears of the groundlings, who for the most part are capable of nothing but inexplicable dumb shows and noise. . . . Be not too tame neither, but let your own discretion be your tutor. Suit the action to the word, the word to the action, with this special observance, that you o'erstep not the modesty of nature. For anything so overdone is from the purpose of playing, whose end, both at the first and now, was and is, to hold, as 'twere, the mirror up to nature, to show virtue her own feature, scorn her own image, and the very age and body of the time his form and pressure. . . . And let those that play your clowns speak no more than is set down for them. . . . Go make you ready.

Hamlet, act 3, scene 2

Clowns should not say more than is set down for them. Let us think about that as we consider a few special comedy techniques. Clowns sometimes get carried away with their own success. This is also true of comedians. It might also be true of you when you are playing a comedy role. What Shakespeare is saying is "Stick to the text—don't try business you haven't rehearsed."

Does this mean a comedian should never ad lib? Certainly not, especially if the comedian is an ad lib artist. Some are. Some are at their best when they are improvising. However, Hamlet is talking to a group of actors who are about to present a play. That makes all the difference. When you are acting in a play, you stay with the script. You might have to ad lib if you go up in your lines, or have to cover for somebody else who has flubbed his lines, and you certainly should be prepared to do just that. However, generally speaking, you say only what is set down for you. You speak the lines the playwright has written, and do only the business you have rehearsed. This is a rule. However, it is a rule that is flexible enough to allow for some spontaneity. Certainly, the essence of comedy is spontaneity. However, it is spontaneity over which the actor must maintain dominion. He must be in command of the situation at all times, and not let the laughter of the crowd tempt him into a kind of clowning that would make his act fall flat.

There are many kinds of comedy. There is everything from slapstick to high comedy, everything from naïveté to sophistication. Basic to all comedy, however, is that special blend of heart and mind. Your heart has to be in what you are doing and saying, but your mind must be in control. It has been said that the best comedians are tragedians at heart. This means they are serious and often secretly sad. They are funny because there is pathos in what they do and say. Their comedy springs from a heart that hurts with compassion. They love the people they entertain and find solace in their laughter.

Yes, but how do they get their laughs? That is what you want to know. There are a few sure-fire tricks. That is where your mind gets into the act. Remember, you must be in command of the situation. You must know what is funny and what is potentially funny. Then you must say the line so it sounds funny. This means rehearsing it until you get the right inflection, until you get the precise rhythm and are punching the key word or words.

When you get a laugh, you wait for it. Nothing is more aggravating to an audience than actors racing on through their lines, never giving people a chance to laugh. Yet this must be done with skill. You cannot simply stop the show and wait for the laugh to die out. You must cover the laugh with business that is in keeping with the situation or with an expression that is in line with your character. However, you do not wait for the laugh to die out entirely. You listen for the peak of the laugh and pick up the dialogue before the laugh dies out.

Comedy calls for precise teamwork. Often the actor who sets things up for a laugh is not the one who speaks the laugh line. Actor A may give all the exposition and Actor B may be the one who says the line or the word which gets the laugh. If Actor A fails at his job, Actor B will likely fail in his. Also it may be a situation in which what Actor B says is funny only because of the way in which Actor A reacts. If Actor A fails to react, Actor B's laugh line falls flat. Comedy is a tricky game of give and take, and the only way to bring it off is with plenty of rehearsing.

There are rules regarding gestures that are especially important to comedy. The fundamental rule is that the gesture should follow the line. If A says to B "You are a fink" and then points his finger at B, he is much more likely to get a laugh than if he points his finger while he is saying the word "fink." Another rule has to do with gesture reversals. Let B threaten A with clenched fists, saying "I'll

break your stubborn jaw." If B then turns away abruptly,
or sinks into a nearby chair, he executes a reverse movement. B is almost certain to get a laugh on the business.
Reversals are universally funny.

Exaggeration, incongruity, and surprise are some of the
other reliable tricks. Notice how Shakespeare uses all three
in Gremio's description of Petruchio's wedding in *The
Taming of the Shrew.*

TRANIO: Signior Gremio, came you from the church?
GREMIO: As willingly as e'er I came from school.
TRANIO: And is the bride and bridegroom coming home?
GREMIO: A bridegroom say you? 'tis a groom indeed,
    A grumbling groom, and that the girl shall find.
TRANIO: Curster than she? why, 'tis impossible.
GREMIO: Why, he's a devil, a devil, a very fiend.
TRANIO: Why, she's a devil, a devil, the devil's dam.
GREMIO: Tut, she's a lamb, a dove, a fool to him!
    I'll tell you, Sir: when the priest
    Should ask, if Katherine should be his wife,
    "Aye, by gog-swounds," quoth he; and swore so loud,
    That, all amazed, the priest let fall the book;
    And, as he stoop'd again to take it up,
    This mad-brain'd bridegroom took him such a cuff,
    That down fell priest and book, and book and priest:
    "Now take them up," quoth he, "if any list."
TRANIO: What said the wench when he rose again?
GREMIO: Trembled and shook; for why he stamp'd and
    swore,
    As if the vicar meant to cozen him.
    But after many ceremonies done,
    He calls for wine: "A health!" quoth he; as if
    He had been aboard, carousing to his mates
    After a storm: quaff'd off the muscadel,
    And threw the sops all in the sexton's face;
    Having no other reason
    But that his beard grew thin and hungerly

And seem'd to ask him sops as he was drinking.
This done, he took the bride about the neck
And kiss'd her lips with such a clamorous smack
That at the parting all the church did echo:
And I seeing this came thence for very shame;
And after me, I know the rout is coming.
Such a mad marriage never was before:
Hark, hark! I hear the minstrels play."
                    The Taming of the Shrew, act 3, scene 2

If you read this Gremio speech straight, it isn't particularly funny. The actor must match the exaggeration, incongruity, and surprise that is in the text with business and line readings. He should dramatize the description of the wedding with descriptive pantomime and vocal mimicry. For example, when he tells how the priest stooped, he should stoop. When he is describing how Petruchio kissed the bride, he should emit a loud smack from his lips.

You can use comedy business to supplement lines. An example of this occurs at the end of *The Taming of the Shrew.* Katherine has just finished her satirical speech to the women, in which she admonishes them to be submissive to their husbands. Then as she says the line "And place your hands below your husband's foot," she does so. Petruchio beams at her, pleased but a little surprised, whereupon Katherine, at the conclusion of her speech, gives Petruchio's foot a yank and throws him backward on his haunches. The stunned Petruchio sits looking at her in a moment of bewilderment, then a smile comes over his face as he says "Why, there's a wench." Then, getting to his feet, and heading for Katherine, he says "Come on, and kiss me, Kate."

Another reliable comedy trick is called parallel business. Two or more actors do exactly the same thing at the same time in the same way. An example of this occurs at the end of Act 1 in Noel Coward's *Hay Fever.* Everyone on stage is having tea. Conversation lags, as it often does when guests are ill at ease. At the end of a long silence, everyone puts his cup in his saucer at the same moment, making a loud click. The business is repeated. Repetition is also good comedy technique. Then, after another silence, two characters start talking at the same time. Embarrassed, they look at each other and break off for another silence. That silence is broken by everybody starting to talk at the same time as the curtain falls. Both parallel business and repetition are used in this instance, but notice that the repetition has variety. Good comedians never repeat a thing more than once or twice without giving it a new twist.

One more tip on how to play comedy—be a good mugger, but never get caught mugging. Mugging is really playing with your face full front to the audience and looking directly into the crowd. That is all right for a vaudeville act or a comedy skit in a musical revue. In a play, however, you should never make direct contact with the audience. The only exceptions to that are presentational moments in which the playwright makes it perfectly clear that the actor is supposed to contact the audience. Such moments do not occur in the average play, so the rule is to keep your eye level just above the heads of the audience. When we advise you to be a good mugger, therefore, we mean only that it is advisable to have your body in an open position when you deliver a punch line. If you play a comedy line in profile and shoot the key words into the wings, you are not likely to get much of a laugh. If, on the other hand, you manage to turn your face slightly toward the audience on the key words, your chance of getting a laugh is greatly enhanced. There are three good reasons for this: 1. When you open to the audience, you give an added emphasis to what you are saying; 2. The audience is more likely to understand you; and 3. The audience can see the expression on your face.

Facial expression is very much a part of putting a comedy line across. In fact, it is so much a part of it there are many comedians who would advise you to practice your comedy lines with one eye on a mirror. If you want to learn how to play comedy, study yourself in a mirror. If you want to learn how to play drama of any kind, study yourself in a mirror. That is the best way to learn the kind of subtlety you need to go from a closed to an open position without being obvious. Mirrors, especially full-length mirrors, can be great aids to actors.

The mirror is so important that we want to give you a quick lesson in how to make it contribute most effectively to your acting. Begin by sitting and looking at yourself in the mirror. Look at your eyes. Study them. See how many different moods you can express by merely changing the expression in your eyes. Now, look at your mouth. Study it. See how many different moods you can express with your mouth alone. Next, study your nose. What can you do with your nose? It isn't so flexible as your mouth, but with a little practice you will be surprised to discover how expressive it can be. Study your forehead and your eyebrows in the same way. Discover how many things you can imply with your eyebrows and your forehead. Now study your whole face. How do you like it? How do you like what you can do with your face?

You may discover that you have one of those faces that are not very mobile. Not good! Not at all good for an actor; what will you do about it? Change it. You can't trade it in for a more expressive face, but you can make it more expressive. You can make it infinitely more expressive. How? Practice.

Practice making faces. Frown, scowl, arch your eyebrows, arch each eyebrow separately. Smile, look happy, look angry, look frightened. Run through the gamut of emotions and study your face. Does your face express what you are feeling? If not, keep working at it. Don't give up. Spend a few minutes every day making faces in the glass. To be sure, making faces isn't acting, but you had better have a face that is mobile enough to do what you want it to do if you want to take acting seriously.

When you've finished with your face, work on your hands in the same way. Look at them. Study them. Hold out your hands with your palms up. Now turn them over with palms down. Think about the different meanings those two positions imply. Hold your hands up as though warding off a blow. Put them together, as in prayer. Lift them above your head as in supplication. Clench your fists. Point your finger, flick your wrists, and do everything that you can think of to make your hands more flexible and more expressive.

Now, study your head, your shoulders, torso, hips, your whole body. See how many crazy angles you can get your body into. Take various stances, various dancing positions. Move mechanically, like a puppet. Move gracefully, like a bird. There, before your mirror, you may discover a whole new world. The world is there, to be discovered. It is your world, and you are to conquer it. When you conquer, when you learn to use your face, your hands, your body to express yourself, you will find that your personality has taken on a new dimension. You will find that you have a new power. Use it wisely. Use it well. Use it with love.

This, then, is how it is done. It is not the whole story. Nevertheless, it is advice you should find useful in the roles you play and in any of the following scenes in which you may perform.

Part II

SELECTED SCENES

Selected Scenes for Testing Skills

The following scenes offer opportunity for the testing of some of the acting skills which have been earlier presented as one of the objectives of this book. Some of the scenes have been chosen with teen-age talent in mind, but most will challenge the students who work on them to reach a little higher than what might be considered their normal age levels.

Anyone with a smattering of talent should be able to perform these scenes, but the idea is to perform them well, and to do well always takes serious effort. Every sportsman knows, as every singer and instrumentalist knows, that the greatest satisfaction from a performance of any kind comes from the feeling that one has done his best. That is the kind of satisfaction students should aim for as they prepare and perform these scenes.

Remembering the basic rules of acting, and applying voice and body techniques, each student should enter into the scene with a goal of excellence, the kind of excellence described in the achievements of the various actors whose lives have been briefly reviewed. All of the scenes here presented may be described as "fun scenes," which means they are fun to do, but the greatest fun comes always from a thing well done. These scenes are followed by a list of additional recommended plays.

Scene from *The Importance of Being Earnest*

A farce by Oscar Wilde
(1 man, 2 women)

In this play the famous satirist Ocar Wilde is ridiculing the hyprocrisy and pretentiousness of Victorian morality. The devious but dapper Jack Worthing wants to marry the charming, sophisticated Gwendolyn, who believes his name to be Earnest, not Jack. She has always wanted to be in love with someone by the name of Earnest, which fact gives us the key to the nonsense which is the essence of the comedy. It is the key also to her superficial character.

The play is highly stylized, which explains the superficiality of all the characters, including Lady Bracknell, whose entrance at a crucial moment accents the farcical aspect of the play and adds to the fun.

Jack (Earnest) and Gwendolyn may play their scene on and around a love seat down right, and there should be a chair for Lady Bracknell just left of center.

The Importance of Being Earnest
by Oscar Wilde

JACK: (*Rises . . . crosses to her right*) Charming day it has been, Miss Fairfax.

GWENDOLYN: Pray don't talk to me about the weather, Mr. Worthing. Whenever people talk to me about the weather, I always feel quite certain that they mean something else. And that makes me so nervous.

JACK: (*Looking back at exit to make sure they are alone*) I do mean something else.

GWENDOLYN: I thought so. In fact, I am never wrong.

JACK: And I would like to be allowed to take advantage of Lady Bracknell's temporary absence . . .

GWENDOLYN: I would certainly advise you to do so. Mamma has a way of coming back suddenly into a room that I have often had to speak to her about.

JACK: (*Nervously*) Miss Fairfax, ever since I met you I have admired you more than any girl. . . . (*Moves to center stage to look at her straight*) I have ever met since . . . I met you. (*Then back closer towards her*)

GWENDOLYN: Yes, I am quite well aware of the fact. And I often wish that in public, at any rate, you had been more demonstrative. For me you have always had an irresistible fascination. Even before I met you I was far from indifferent to you.

(*Jack looks at her in amazement*)

We live, as I hope you know, Mr. Worthing, in an age of ideals. The fact is constantly mentioned in the more expensive monthly magazines, and has reached the provincial pulpits, I am told; and my ideal has always been to love some one of the name of Earnest. There is something in that name that inspires absolute confidence. The moment Algernon first mentioned to me that he had a friend called Earnest, I knew I was destined to love you.

JACK: (*Hand on hers*) You really love me, Gwendolyn?

GWENDOLYN: Passionately!!

JACK: Darling! You don't know how happy you've made me.

GWENDOLYN: My own Earnest!

JACK: But you don't really mean to say that you couldn't love me if my name wasn't Earnest?

GWENDOLYN: But your name is Earnest.

JACK: (*Up from squatting position*) Yes, I know it is. But supposing it was something else? Do you mean to say you couldn't love me then?

GWENDOLYN: (*Glibly*) Ah! That is clearly a metaphysical speculation, and like most metaphysical speculations has very little reference at all to the actual facts of real life, as we know them.

JACK: (*Crossing slowly to back of chair*) Personally, darling, to speak quite candidly, I don't much care about the name of Earnest. . . . I don't think the name suits me at all.

GWENDOLYN: It suits you perfectly. It is a divine name. It has music of its own. It produces vibrations.

JACK: Well, really, Gwendolyn, I must say that I think there are lots of other much nicer names. (*Cross back to her left*) I think Jack, for instance, a charming name.

GWENDOLYN: Jack? . . . No, there is very little music in the name Jack, if any at all, indeed. It does not thrill. It produces absolutely no vibrations. . . . I have known several Jacks, and they all, without exception, were more than usually plain. Besides, Jack is a notorious domesticity for John and I pity any woman who is married to a man called John. She would probably never be allowed to know the entrancing pleasure of a single moment's solitude. The only really safe name is Earnest.

JACK: (*Cross D.L. 2*) Gwendolyn, I must get christened at

once. . . . I mean we must get married at once. There is no time to be lost.

GWENDOLYN: Married, Mr. Worthing?

JACK: (*Astounded*) Well . . . surely. You know that I love you, and you led me to believe, Miss Fairfax, that you were not absolutely indifferent to me.

GWENDOLYN: I adore you. But you haven't proposed to me yet. Nothing has been said at all about marriage. The subject has not even been touched on.

JACK: Well . . . may I propose to you now?

GWENDOLYN: I think it would be an admirable opportunity. And to spare you any possible disappointment, Mr. Worthing, I think it only fair to tell you quite frankly beforehand that I am fully determined to accept you.

JACK: Gwendolyn! (*Around back of chair to her right*)

GWENDOLYN: Yes, Mr. Worthing, what have you got to say to me?

JACK: You know what I have got to say to you.

GWENDOLYN: Yes, but you don't say it.

JACK: (*On one knee, hand on hers*) Gwendolyn, will you marry me?

GWENDOLYN: Of course I will, darling. How long you have been about it! I am afraid you have had very little experience in how to propose.

JACK: My own one, I have never loved any one in the world but you.

GWENDOLYN: Yes, but men often propose for practice. I know my brother Gerald does. All my girl friends tell me so. What wonderfully blue eyes you have, Earnest! They are quite, quite blue. I hope you will always look at me just like that, especially when there are other people present.

(*Enter Lady Bracknell*)

LADY BRACKNELL: Mr. Worthing! Rise, sir, from this semi-recumbent posture. It is most indecorous.

GWENDOLYN: Mamma!

(*He tries to rise, but from surprise falls all over himself and Gwendolyn is no help at all*)
I must beg you to retire. This is no place for you. Besides, Mr. Worthing has not quite finished yet.

LADY BRACKNELL: Finished what, may I ask?

GWENDOLYN: I am engaged to Mr. Worthing, Mamma.
(*Both of them finally get up on this line*)

LADY BRACKNELL: Pardon me, you are not engaged to any one. (*Puts books and other stuff in the chair to the right. X to D.R. 2*) When you do become engaged to some one, I, or your father, should his health permit him, will inform you of the fact. An engagement should come on a young girl as a surprise, pleasant or unpleasant, as the case may be. It is hardly a matter that she could be allowed to arrange for herself. . . . And now I have a few questions to put to you, Mr. Worthing. While I am making these inquiries, you, Gwendolyn, will wait for me below in the carriage.

GWENDOLYN: (*Reproachfully*) Mamma!

LADY BRACKNELL: In the carriage, Gwendolyn!
(*Gwendolyn goes to the door. She and Jack blow kisses to each other behind Lady Bracknell's back. Lady Bracknell looks vaguely as if she could not understand what the noise was. Finally she turns around*)
Gwendolyn, the carriage!

GWENDOLYN: Yes, mamma. (*Goes out looking back at Jack*)

LADY BRACKNELL: (*Sitting down in U.R. chair*) You can take a seat, Mr. Worthing.
(*Looks in her pocket for notebook and pencil*)

JACK: Thank you, Lady Bracknell, I prefer standing.
(*Moves a little down stage of chair*)

LADY BRACKNELL: (*Pencil and notebook in hand*) I feel bound to tell you that you are not down on my list of eligible young men although I have the same list as the dear Duchess of Bolton has. We work together,

in fact. However, I am quite ready to enter your
name, should your answers be what a really affec-
tionate mother requires. Do you smoke?

JACK: Well, yes, I admit I smoke. (*Rather worried and
concerned*)

LADY BRACKNELL: I am glad to hear it. A man should always have an occupation of some kind. There are far
too many idle men in London as it is. How old are
you?

JACK: Twenty-nine.

LADY BRACKNELL: A very good age to be married at. I have
always been of the opinion that a man who desires to
get married should know either everything or nothing. Which do you know?

JACK: (*After some hesitation*) I know nothing, Lady
Bracknell.

LADY BRACKNELL: I am pleased to hear it. I do not approve
of anything that tampers with natural ignorance.
Ignorance is like a delicate exotic fruit; touch it and
the bloom is gone. The whole theory of modern education is radically unsound. Fortunately in England,
at any rate, education produces no effect whatsoever.
If it did, it would prove a serious danger to the upper
classes, and probably lead to acts of violence in Gros-
venor Square. What is your income?

JACK: Between seven and eight thousand a year. (*Pacing
nervously*)

LADY BRACKNELL: (*Makes a note in her book*) In land or
in investments?

JACK: In investments chiefly. (*Straightens jacket . . .
pleased*)

LADY BRACKNELL: That is satisfactory. What between the
duties expected of one during one's lifetime, and the
duties exacted from one after one's death, land has
ceased to be either a profit or a pleasure. It gives one
position and prevents one from keeping it up. That's
all that can be said about land.

JACK: I have a country house with some land, of course, attached to it, about fifteen hundred acres, I believe; but I don't depend on that for my real income. In fact, as far as I can make out, the poachers are the only people who make anything out of it.

LADY BRACKNELL: A country house! How many bedrooms? Well, that point can be cleared up afterwards. You have a town house, I hope? A girl with a simple, unspoiled nature, like Gwendolyn, could hardly be expected to reside in the country.

JACK: Well, I own a house in Belgrave Square, but it is let by the year to Lady Bloxham. Of course, I can get it back whenever I like, at six month's notice. (*Reassuringly*)

LADY BRACKNELL: Lady Bloxham? I don't know her.

JACK: Oh, she goes about very little. She is a lady considerably advanced in years.

LADY BRACKNELL: Ah, nowadays that is no guarantee of respectability of character. What number in Belgrave Square?

JACK: 149.

LADY BRACKNELL: (*Shaking her head*) The unfashionable side. I thought there was something. However, that could easily be altered.

JACK: Do you mean the fashion, or the side?

LADY BRACKNELL: (*Sternly*) Both, if necessary, I presume. What are your politics?

JACK: Well, I am afraid I really have none. I am a Liberal Unionist.

LADY BRACKNELL: Oh, they count as Tories. They dine with us. Or come in the evening, at any rate. Now to minor matters. Are your parents living?

JACK: I have lost both my parents.

LADY BRACKNELL: To lose one parent, Mr. Worthing, may be regarded as a misfortune; to lose both looks like carelessness. Who was your father? He was evidently a man of some wealth. Was he born in what the Radical papers call the purple of commerce, or did he rise from the ranks of the aristocracy?

JACK: I am afraid I really don't know. The fact is, Lady Bracknell, I said I had lost my parents. It would be nearer the truth to say that my parents seem to have lost me. . . . I don't actually know who I am by birth. I was . . . well, I was found. (*Reluctantly*)

LADY BRACKNELL: Found!

JACK: The late Mr. Thomas Cardew, an old gentleman of a very charitable and kindly disposition, found me, and gave me the name of Worthing, because he happened to have a first-class ticket for Worthing in his pocket at the time. Worthing is a place in Sussex. It is a seaside resort.

LADY BRACKNELL: Where did the charitable gentleman who had a first-class ticket for this seaside resort find you?

JACK: (*Gravely*) In a hand-bag.

LADY BRACKNELL: (*Even more appalled*) A hand-bag?

JACK: (*Very seriously and gesturing in an effort to explain*) Yes, Lady Bracknell. I was in a hand-bag . . . a somewhat large, black leather hand-bag, with handles on it . . . an ordinary hand-bag, in fact.

LADY BRACKNELL: In what locality did this Mr. James or Thomas Cardew come across this ordinary hand-bag?

JACK: In the cloak-room at Victoria Station. It was given to him in mistake for his own.

LADY BRACKNELL: The cloak-room at Victoria Station?

JACK: Yes. The Brighton Line.

LADY BRACKNELL: The line is immaterial. Mr. Worthing, I confess I feel somewhat bewildered by what you have just told me. To be born, or at any rate bred, in a hand-bag, whether it had handles or not, seems to me to display a contempt for the ordinary decencies of family life that reminds one of the worst excesses of the French Revolution. And I presume you know what that unfortunate movement led to? As for the particular locality in which the hand-bag was found, a cloak-room at a railway station might serve to conceal a social indiscretion . . . has probably, indeed, been used for that purpose before now . . . but it could hardly be regarded as an assured basis for a recognized position in good society.

JACK: May I ask you then what you would advise me to do? I need hardly say I would do anything in the world to ensure Gwendolyn's happiness.

LADY BRACKNELL: (*Rising*) I would strongly advise you, Mr. Worthing, to try and acquire some relations as soon as possible and to make a definite effort to produce, at any rate, one parent, of either sex, before the season is quite over.

JACK: Well, I don't see how I could possibly manage to do that. I can produce the hand-bag at any moment. It is in my dressing-room at home. I really think that should satisfy you, Lady Bracknell.

LADY BRACKNELL: Me, sir! What has it to do with me? You can hardly imagine that I and Lord Bracknell would dream of allowing our only daughter . . . a girl brought up with the utmost care . . . to marry into a cloak-room, and form an alliance with a parcel. Good morning, Mr. Worthing!

(*Lady Bracknell sweeps out in majestic indignation . . . up center*)

JACK: (*Plopping down in the U.L. chair with a thud*) Good morning!!

Scene from *Man Like Lincoln*

A drama by Albert Johnson
(1 man, 1 woman)

Abe Lincoln, shy but obviously falling in love, waltzes awkwardly on from stage left with the pretty, flirtatious, graceful Mary Todd. This is a comedy scene from an otherwise serious play. It should be played for the inherent humor, but with a strong hint of those character traits that enable Abraham Lincoln to become the strong man of compassion that he was. In Mary we should see traits of the scheming, willful woman she became.

The scene may be played on a bare stage.

Man Like Lincoln
by Albert Johnson

(*Mary and Abe are dancing*)

MARY: (*Laughing*) I declare, Mr. Lincoln! You dance like a polar bear!

ABE: (*As they break the step and stand regarding each other*) A polar bear, Miss Mary, would know how to break the ice.

MARY: Have I been that cold, Mr. Lincoln?

ABE: It's just that I never know quite what to say, I reckon.

MARY: You listen, and that's a sure way to win a woman's interest, Mr. Lincoln.

ABE: Yours, Miss Mary?

MARY: Thank you for the flowers, Mr. Lincoln. Lilacs always remind me of Kentucky.

ABE: It's kinda odd, my being here. I don't belong in high society, a country lawyer, a small-time politician, but people draw me, like a light draws millers.

MARY: You might say I don't belong in Springfield, but I'm glad I came.

ABE: Why did you come, Miss Mary?

MARY: My sister says, to catch a man.

ABE: *(After a chuckle)* That won't be hard, I reckon, excepting that he'd better be somebody mighty tolerable; a judge, or congressman, at least.

MARY: Oh, no. The man I marry will be President of the United States.

ABE: *(Seriously, after a chuckle)* Good night, Miss Mary, I'll not be seeing you again, I reckon. It's best I don't.
(They drift apart, as the lights fade to indicate a passage of time)
(Lights up to reveal Abe waving to unseen person off left. Mary enters down right)

VOICE OFF LEFT: Well, Abe, y' kinda shook things up. I reckon everybody in Missouri's waitin' t' shake hands with ya. But I jes' wanna say I wish we had men like you in our Missouri legislature.

ABE: *(His face lighting up at sight of Mary)* Miss Mary! I had no idea you were here.

MARY: I'm quite surprised myself, Mr. Lincoln. That was a great speech, Mr. Lincoln. Oh, but I'm keeping you from all your admirers, Mr. Lincoln.

ABE: Will you go for a little walk with me?

MARY: Yes, Mr. Lincoln. *(They smile at each other)*

ABE: Where shall we walk to? That hill up yonder? We could watch the sun go down.

MARY: All right. (*They start to cross toward U.R. and Mary trips over an imaginary stone*)

ABE: (*Taking her arm*) I'm sorry, Miss Mary. Here, let me take your arm. I guess I'm more used to walking a plowed field alone than I am walking with young ladies.

MARY: You forget what long legs you have, Mr. Lincoln.

ABE: Well, if I go too fast, you holler "Whoa."

MARY: (*As they reach a position U.R.*) Whoa!

ABE: (*As they pause to look about*) You can see the tops of trees up here, all scarlet and soft gold.

MARY: Do you ever feel that you'd like to gather this great, vast, beauteous land into your arms and hold it to your heart?

ABE: (*Looking at her in wonder*) You have ideas like that, too!

MARY: Moments like this, I tremble at the wonder that is America.

ABE: I'd like to have legs long enough to step from the Mississippi clean to the Rockies.

MARY: Your legs, Mr. Lincoln, are quite long enough! (*They both laugh*)

ABE: (*Growing serious after they have stood for a moment in silence*) Mary, how old are you?

MARY: (*Surprised*) You've never called me that before . . . just . . . Mary.

ABE: I hope you don't mind. It's a good name . . . Mary . . .

MARY: I'm twenty-one.

ABE: You'd think that by the time a man reached thirty, he'd know what it was he ought to do in life. I'm thirty-one. I reckon there's a big difference between us. Not just our ages only. Other men seem to know just what they want in life.

MARY: Judge Logan says you're doing well at law. And the way that crowd cheered you today!

ABE: I reckon what I want most is just to be around people, all kinds of people. But they're always sayin' 'What're y' aimin' to make of yourself, Abe?' So I finally started on law, mostly to please my friends, I reckon.

MARY: Law opens many avenues, and so do politics.

ABE: Maybe what I need is a good, swift kick. Any other man, standing where I'm standing, would be talking about you, not about himself.

MARY: That might get boring.

ABE: Not to me. Not to any man who could find his tongue enough to say how pretty you look. The red, red sun making you all rosy . . .

MARY: Maybe that's because you've torn down the wall.

ABE: The wall?

MARY: The wall you always seem to put between us.

ABE: And I always thought it was you who put the wall there. (*Thoughtfully, after a silence.*) Twenty-one. Girls twenty-one generally think about getting married.

MARY: And men thirty-one think about what they ought to do in life.

ABE: (*After a silence*) Maybe . . . maybe we can help each other make up our minds.

MARY: Maybe we can.

ABE: I reckon I've not got much to offer a girl like you. But there's never been . . . there'll never be another . . . I'd want so much . . . to ask to be my wife.

MARY: (*After a pause, almost afraid to ask it*) Do you . . . love me, Mr. Lincoln?

ABE: I don't have words for saying it the way I'd like, but if you're willing, I'll show you all my life. So . . . are you willing?

MARY: (*Jubilantly*) Yes, Mr. Lincoln! Even if you never get to be President of the United States!

3

Scene from *Pierre Patelin*

An old French farce. Author unknown.
(2 men)

One of the funniest of all farces is the short play entitled
Pierre Patelin. An unscrupulous scalawag by that name
cons a muddle-minded merchant out of a piece of fine
goods, which he means to have tailored into splendid gar-
ments for himself and his wife. The fruits of thievery are
the seeds of travail, as the ensuing complications demonstrate.

The scene that follows occurs early in the play. A table
down left may serve as the merchant's counter. Pierre
enters right to address the merchant, who is behind his
counter.

Pierre Patelin
Anonymous

PATELIN: (*Peering into the Draper's shop*) Not there? . . .
H'm! Yes, there he is. . . . Aye, he's busy with his
goods. (*While Patelin is reconnoitering, the Draper*

emerges and lays several rolls of goods on his counter. Then, on looking up, he spies Patelin, who greets him with a beguiling smile.) My dear sir, God bless you!

GUILLAUME,

THE DRAPER: And give you joy!

PATELIN: (*Leaning his hands on the counter*) I've been longing to see you, Guillaume. How's your health? You're feeling fine?

THE DRAPER: Aye, that I am!

PATELIN: (*Holding out his hand.*) There! (*A pause*) How goes it?

THE DRAPER: Why, first rate! . . . And how are you?

PATELIN: (*Giving the Draper a friendly clap on the shoulder*) By Saint Peter, never better! . . . So you're feeling cheerful, eh?

THE DRAPER: To be sure. But merchants, you must know, have their troubles.

PATELIN: How is business? It yields enough, I trust, to keep the pot a-boiling?

THE DRAPER: Afore Heaven, my good sir, I hardly know. (*Imitating the cluck of a driver to his horse*) I manage to get along! (*He sighs*)

PATELIN: (*In a reminiscent reverie*) Ah, he was a knowing one!—your father was, I mean. God rest his soul! (*Scanning the Draper with amazement*) I can hardly believe I'm not looking at him now! What a merchant he was! and clever? . . . I swear, you're the very picture of him. . . . If God was ever moved to pity, may he grant your father his soul's pardon! (*Takes off his hat and glances piously toward heaven. The Draper follows suit.*)

THE DRAPER: (*Sanctimoniously*) Amen! Through his mercy! And ours, too, when it shall please him! (*Both replace their hats.*)

PATELIN: (*With a touch of melancholy*) Ah, yes! Many a time he foretold me the days that we are come to. I've

often thought of it. (*After a slight pause*) He was one
of the good . . .

THE DRAPER: (*Interrupting Patelin's reminiscences by of-
fering him a seat*) Do sit down, sir. I should have
asked you before. (*Self-reproachful*) A thousand
pardons!

PATELIN: (*As if his own comfort were of no importance*)
Tut, tut, man! I'm all right. . . . He used to . . . (*Another interruption by the Draper, who, in his zeal to
show good manners to a prospective customer, leans
over his counter as far as he can, grasps Patelin by the
shoulders, and endeavors to force him to sit down.*)

THE DRAPER: Oh, do sit down.

PATELIN: (*Yielding*) Gladly. (*A short pause, after which
Patelin blithely resumes his yarn*) "Oh," says he to
me, "you'll see marvelous things!" . . . I'll take my
oath! ears, nose, mouth, eyes,—no child was ever so
like his father. (*Pointing*) That dimpled chin! Why,
it's him to a dot! I can't imagine how ever Nature
made two so similar faces! Why, look! If you had both
been spat against a wall in the selfsame manner and
in one array, you wouldn't differ by a hair. But, sir,
good Laurentia, your step-aunt, is she still living?

THE DRAPER: (*Mystified*) Why, yes!

PATELIN: (*Rising*) How comely she seemed to me, and tall,
and straight, and full of graces! . . . And you take after
her in figure, as if they'd copied her. No family here-
abouts comes up to yours for likenesses. The more I
see you, . . . Bless my soul! (*Pointing to a mirror*)
Look at yourself. You're looking at your father! (*Clapping the Draper on the back with jovial familiarity*)
You resemble him closer than a drop of water! . . .
What a mettlesome blade he was! the worthy man,—
and trusted every one. Heaven forgive him! He always
used to laugh so heartily with me. Would to God
more people resembled him! There'd be less wicked-

ness. (*Feeling a piece of cloth*) How well made this cloth is! how smooth it is, and soft, and nicely woven!

THE DRAPER: (*Proudly*) I had it made to order from the wool of my own flock.

PATELIN: (*Overflowing with admiration*) You don't say so! What a manager you are! (*Jocularly*) It's your father all over again. Blood will tell! . . . (*Awestruck*) You're always, always busy.

THE DRAPER: (*Solemnly*) One must be! To get a living a man must be shrewd and enterprising.

PATELIN: (*Handling another piece of goods*) Was this piece dyed in the wool? It's as strong as leather.

THE DRAPER: (*Showing off the weave of his goods*) That's Rouen goods, and well fulled, I promise you.

PATELIN: Now, upon my word, I'm caught by that. I had no thought of getting cloth when I came, by my soul, I hadn't. I'd laid aside some four score crowns for an investment, but twenty or thirty of them will fall to you.

THE DRAPER: Crowns, you say?

PATELIN: (*Picking up the cloth again*) What kind of goods is this, you say? . . . The more I see it, the sillier it makes me. I must have a coat of that,—and another for my wife.

THE DRAPER: Cloth costs like holy oil.

PATELIN: I don't care: give me my money's worth. In a word, I'm hot for this piece, and have some I must.

THE DRAPER: Right! But first how much do you want? . . . Though you hadn't a brass farthing, the whole pile is at your service.

PATELIN: (*Gazing rather absent-mindedly at the cloth*) I know that well, thank you.

THE DRAPER: You might like some of this sky-colored stuff?

PATELIN: First, how much is a single yard to cost? (*On saying this, Patelin holds up a penny so that the Draper may get a good look at it*) Here's a penny to seal the bargain in God's name; God's share shall be paid first: that stands to reason. (*Piously doffs his hat, strides solemnly to a box set up in the market-place for receiving God's pennies, drops the coin in, and returns to the Draper.*)

THE DRAPER: That's the way to talk! You want the bottom price?

PATELIN: Yes.

THE DRAPER: (*Decisively*) It will cost you four and twenty pence a yard.

PATELIN: Go to! Four and twenty pence! Heaven save us!

THE DRAPER: (*Laying his hand on his heart*) I cross my heart! it cost me every whit of that, and I can't afford to lose.

PATELIN: Lord! it's too much.

THE DRAPER: You'd never believe how cloth has risen! This winter the livestock all perished in the great frost.

PATELIN: But twenty pence! twenty pence!

THE DRAPER: No, sir! Twenty-four. Not a farthing less!

PATELIN: Very well, then! I'll buy without further haggling. Come, measure off!

THE DRAPER: And pray, how much must you have?

PATELIN: (*As if to himself, and cocking his head without looking at the Draper*) For me, three yards, and for her—she's tall—two and a half. In all, six yards. . . . Why, no, that's not right! How stupid of me! Let's see.

THE DRAPER: There wants but half a yard to make the six.

PATELIN: Give me the even six, then. I need a hat as well.

THE DRAPER: (*Pointing to the other end of his strip of cloth*) Take hold there. We'll measure. Here they are, and no scrimping. (*He measures, and each time he lets go, Patelin cheats by pulling the cloth a little toward himself.*) One, . . . and two, . . . and three, . . . and four, . . . and five, . . . and six!

PATELIN: By Saint Peter! Measured close!

THE DRAPER: (*Looking at Patelin, then turning his ell in*

the other direction. Naïvely) Shall I measure back again?

PATELIN: (*With cheerful disdain*) Oh, dear no! There's always a little gain or loss. How much does it all amount to?

THE DRAPER: Let's see. At four and twenty pence, each,— for the six yards, nine francs.

PATELIN: (*Aside*) Hm! Here goes! (*To the Draper*) Six crowns?

THE DRAPER: Yes.

PATELIN: Now, sir, will you trust me for 'em? . . . until presently, when you come? (*The Draper shows symptoms of suspicion*) No, I don't mean trust. I'll pay cash—good for anything you say—at my house.

THE DRAPER: (*Ungraciously*) That's off my road.

PATELIN: (*With playful irony*) By my lord Saint Giles, now you're telling gospel truth! Off your road! That's it! You're never ready to drink at my house, but this is the time you shall!

THE DRAPER: Good Lord! I'm always drinking! (*After a moment's hesitation*) I'll come; but let me tell you it's against my principles to give credit on a first sale, like this.

PATELIN: What if I pay for it, not in silver or copper, but in good yellow coin? (*Craftily*) Oho! and you must have a bit of that goose my wife is roasting!

THE DRAPER: (*Aside*) The man drives me mad. (*Aloud*) Go on! Away! I will follow you, and bring the cloth.

PATELIN: (*Who by this time has picked up the bundle of goods*) Not at all! Not at all! It's no trouble. It isn't heavy! I can carry it myself. See! Under my arm. . . . So!

THE DRAPER: (*Trying to recover his property*) No, indeed, sir! it would look better for me to bring it.

PATELIN: (*Tucking the cloth into his long gown*) I'll be hanged if you do! See how snug it lies, here, under

my elbow. What a jolly hump it will give me! Ah!
now it's all right! (*With mock hilarity*) We'll have a
fling before you leave.

THE DRAPER: And I shall get my money as soon as I've
arrived?

PATELIN: You shall that! But no! First you shall dine! I'm
glad I have no cash about me now. (*Archly*) At least
you'll come and try my wine, now won't you? When
your late father went by my house he used to sing
out, "Hullo, friend!" or, "What's the good word" or,
"How do you do," But you don't care a straw for poor
folk, you rich men!

THE DRAPER: (*Flattered but deprecatory*) Oh, now, see
here, we're the poor ones!

PATELIN: (*Laughing incredulously*) Whew! Well, goodbye, goodbye! Turn up soon, and we'll have a good
drink. Count on that.

THE DRAPER: All right! Go ahead, then, and see that I'm
paid in gold! (*Patelin starts homeward. The Draper
disappears within his shop.*)

PATELIN: (*Crosses to L. of the market-place.*) Gold! H'm!
Gold! The devil! I made no slips that time! (*Overcome by a sense of immense absurdity, Patelin stops
once or twice to laugh gaily and derisively at the mere
idea of paying anything—especially in gold.*) No! gold!
I'd see him hanged. (*Chuckling*) He set his own
price, but he shall get mine! He must have gold, must
he? He shall get it—ha! ha! Would he might run without stopping till he's paid! (*Enters the alley L.U. and
disappears.*)

THE DRAPER: (*Coming out again*) Those crowns of his—
I'll take care of them! It takes two to make a bargain.
That scalawag pays four and twenty pence a yard for
cloth that's not worth twenty!

4

Scene from *People are Talking*

A comedy by Albert Johnson
(2 men)

Even a nice guy sometimes has trouble trying to do the right thing for the right reason. Being hooked with a name like "Junior" can be trouble enough, but Junior wants something. He wants it so badly he can hear it bark. Just a few bucks will buy that dog he wants.

Suddenly there is Brute, his best pal, practically handing him the money. But Brute has a scheme that sounds a little wild. Will it work? Is it right? Is Brute being taken for a ride?

Unlike some of the other scenes, this one gives the actors a chance to work with ordinary, everyday conversation. It may be played on a bare stage.

People Are Talking
by Albert Johnson

BRUTE: (*Wheeling in from left*) Well, it's about time. Did you get my message?

JUNIOR: How could I miss it? You wrote it on every blackboard in the administration building.

BRUTE: Well, that just shows you how important it is. That I see you, I mean.

JUNIOR: O.K. Brute. What's the pitch?

BRUTE: Sure nobody's listening? Maybe we ought to step inside.

JUNIOR: Inside? Then we would have an audience.

BRUTE: (*Confidentially*) Well, this guy comes up to me, see, and he says do I know any way he can get into the high school office tomorrow afternoon on account of he's got to do some repair work on the safe. So I says why don't you see the principal, Mr. McAulay? So he says unfortunately he got out of town for the week-end and so did his secretary before he had a chance to arrange to get in.

JUNIOR: Yeah, that's true. They are gone for the week-end.

BRUTE: So then he says do I know the janitor. And I say you mean the main janitor, Pop Percival, or the student janitor who has charge of the principal's office?

JUNIOR: So then what?

BRUTE: Well, he (*He imitates the man*) he kinda chuckles and says no, no sense him bothering the old man just for a little thing like that on account he knows Pop Percival's got more than he can handle, so do I know the student janitor and I says sure, he's my best buddy, and then I told him about you 'cause I knew you just got the job today.

JUNIOR: Yeah, that's right. So I can earn money for a St. Bernard puppy, and oh boy, Brute, you ought to see him! He's all feet and ears and when I left him to go back to algebra, which I incidentally didn't go back to, he howled like a baby.

BRUTE: Yeah, well, that's swell, but about this guy—

JUNIOR: The trouble is, Brute, about the St. Bernard, I mean. If I don't get thirty-five bucks by tomorrow he's very likely to be sold to someone else. That's what the man at the kennels said.

BRUTE: Well, if you'll shut up and listen to the rest of what I'm trying to tell you, you can maybe make that thirty-five bucks and more.

JUNIOR: How? For Pete's sake, how?

BRUTE: Well, this guy, see, that wants to do some work on the high school safe—well, he says it's awful important to him and his outfit that he get into the office tomorrow afternoon and that it's so important that he will pay me fifty bucks if I can arrange with the student janitor, that's you, to let him in tomorrow at 4:00 P.M.

JUNIOR: Fifty bucks? He'll pay me fifty dollars to let him in the principal's office?

BRUTE: He'll pay *me* fifty dollars if I can arrange it, but I'll split it with you, see?

JUNIOR: Wait a minute. How do we know this guy is on the level? How do we know he's not a safe-cracker or something?

BRUTE: Yeah, I wondered about that too, but he showed me his, what-do-you-call-'em—his credentials, some papers and stuff. They looked pretty official to me, and besides he said just to prove to me he was on the level he'd pay me ten dollars in advance.

JUNIOR: And did he?

BRUTE: (*Taking bills from his pocket*) Sure. I got it right here. Five ones and a five. Nice crisp bills.

JUNIOR: I don't know, Brute. Sounds kinda fishy. I mean if this guy really does work for some big safe repair company, well wouldn't the company arrange with Mr. McAulay?

BRUTE: Yeah, but the man said there was some sort of mix-up in the head office. You know how those things are.

JUNIOR: Yeah, fifty bucks. Gee.

BRUTE: Twenty-five. You got to split with me, remember.

JUNIOR: Gee, then I'd only need ten more to get that St. Bernard pup. No, I wouldn't either. Jeepers! I was forgetting. I sold my bike this afternoon for twelve-fifty. Tell you what, Brute, I'll see you tomorrow about this deal. Come over first thing.

BRUTE: Yeah. O.K.

JUNIOR: First thing tomorrow.

Permission to use granted by The Heuer Publishing Company, Cedar Rapids, Iowa, 1948.

5

Scene from *The Taming of the Shrew*

A comedy by William Shakespeare
(1 man, 1 woman)

When Petruchio and Katherine meet it is love at first sight. Actors playing the roles must begin with that premise. This is important, because nothing in the dialogue seems to support that fact. On the contrary, it is a war of wits from their first encounter.

Petruchio, a swaggering, strutting young cock, is out to win a wife. Katherine, a beautiful but foul-tempered, willful wench, will not be easily won. The fight is on, and the sparks that fly between them are from the very magnet that basically draws them together. The scene, which may be done on a bare stage, is a spicy example of sparkling repartee at its best.

Petruchio is down right as Katherine enters up left.

The Taming of the Shrew
by William Shakespeare

PETRUCHIO: Good morrow, Kate, for that's your name I hear.

KATE: Well have you heard, but something hard of hearing. They call me Katherine, that do talk of me.

PETRUCHIO: You lie in faith, for you are called plain Kate,
And bonny Kate, and sometimes Kate the curst:
But Kate, the prettiest Kate in Christendom,
Kate of Kate-Hall, my super-dainty Kate,
For dainties are all cates, and therefore Kate,
Take this of me, Kate of my consolation,
Hearing thy mildness prais'd in every town,
Thy virtue spoke of, and thy beauty sounded,
Yet not so deeply as to thee belongs,
Myself am mov'd to woo thee for my wife.

KATE: Mov'd, in good time! Let him that mov'd you hither
Remove you hence. I knew you at the first you were
a moveable.

PETRUCHIO: Why, what's a moveable?

KATE: A join'd stool.

PETRUCHIO: Thou hast hit it; come sit on me.

KATE: Asses are made to bear, and so are you.

PETRUCHIO: Women are made to bear, and so are you.

KATE: No such jade as you, if me you mean.

PETRUCHIO: Alas good Kate, I will not burden thee,
For knowing thee to be but young and light . . .

KATE: Too light for such a swain as you to catch
And yet as heavy as my weight should be.

PETRUCHIO: Should be, should: buzz!

KATE: Well taken, and like a buzzard.

PETRUCHIO: O slow-winged turtle, shall a buzzard take
thee?

KATE: Ay, for a turtle, as he takes a buzzard.

PETRUCHIO: Come, come, you wasp; in faith, you are
too angry.

KATE: If I be waspish, best beware my sting.

PETRUCHIO: My remedy is then to pluck it out.

KATE: Ay, if the fool could find it where it lies.

PETRUCHIO: Who knows not where a wasp does wear his
sting? In his tail.

KATE: In his tongue!

PETRUCHIO: Whose tongue?

KATE: Yours, if you talk of tales, and so farewell.

PETRUCHIO: Nay, come again, good Kate, I am a gentleman.
   Kate, you must not look so sour.

KATE: It is my fashion when I see a crab.

PETRUCHIO: Why, here's no crab, and therefore look not
   sour.

KATE: There is, there is!

PETRUCHIO: Then show it me.

KATE: Had I a glass, I would.

PETRUCHIO: What, you mean my face?

KATE: Well aim'd, of such a young one.

PETRUCHIO: Now, by Saint George, I am too young for you.

KATE: Yet, you are wither'd.

PETRUCHIO: 'Tis with cares.

KATE: I care not.

PETRUCHIO: Nay, hear you, Kate. In sooth you 'scape not so.
   (*As Kate starts to leave he grabs her, and they struggle*)

KATE: I chafe you if I tarry. Let me go!

PETRUCHIO: No, not a whit, I find you passing gentle:
   It was told me you were rough, and coy, and sullen,
   And now I find report a very liar:
   (*Kate stamps her foot and struggles*)
   For thou art pleasant, gamesome, passing courteous,
   But slow in speech: yet sweet as spring-time flowers.
   Thou canst not frown, thou canst not look askance,
   Nor bite the lip as angry wenches will,
   Nor hast thou pleasure to be cross in talk,
   But thou with mildness entertain'st thy wooers,
   With gentle conference, soft, and affable.
   (*Kate breaks from him, moving quickly*)
   Why does the world report that Kate doth limp?
   (*Kate stops abruptly*)
   Oh let me see thee walk: thou dost not halt.

KATE: Go, fool, and whom thou keep'st command.

PETRUCHIO: Did ever Dian so become a grove

As Kate this chamber with her princely gait:
O be thou Dian, and let her be Kate,
And then let Kate be chaste, and Dian sportful.

KATE: Where did you study all this goodly speech?

PETRUCHIO: It is extempore, from the mother wit.

KATE: A witty mother, witless else her son.

PETRUCHIO: Am I not wise?

KATE: Yes, keep you warm.

PETRUCHIO: Marry so I mean, sweet Katherine, in thy bed:
(*He crosses quickly to her and holds her firmly*)
And therefore setting all this chat aside
Thus in plain terms: your father hath consented
That you shall be my wife; your dowry 'greed on,
And will you, nill you, I will marry you!
(*Petruchio kisses Kate*)

6

Scene from *The School for Husbands*

by Molière
(2 men, 1 woman)

Sganarelle, self-deceiving old curmudgeon, is raising his young ward, Isabelle, to be his wife. Although he guards her like a despot, she obviously has a mind of her own, and she is, quite knowingly and willingly, the object of Valère's affections.

Valère, a young, handsome dandy, lives next door and is handy for secret meetings and for the deceptive flirtation which they engage in before the very eyes of the credulous Sganarelle.

This scene must be played with high style, with lines and actions exaggerated. The fun is in the double entendre (double meaning) bantered back and forth when the three are together. It may be played on a bare stage.

The School for Husbands
by Molière

SGANARELLE: (*To Valère*) One moment. *You're* the man I'm looking for!

VALÈRE: (*Bowing*) Delighted!

SGANARELLE: I want a word with you.

VALÈRE: Indeed! Come inside.

SGANARELLE: I prefer the street.

VALÈRE: But the noise?——

SGANARELLE: I hear well.

VALÈRE: Will you sit down?

SGANARELLE: I'll stand. I'm quite at ease.

VALÈRE: *(Aside)* The gentleman is difficult to please.

SGANARELLE: You know that I'm the guardian of a . . . well,
A rather pretty girl, named Isabelle,
Who lives nearby?

VALÈRE: Yes.

SGANARELLE: And do you know
That since her dying father willed it so,
When I shall give the word, she marries me?

VALÈRE: No. That's too bad!

SGANARELLE: What's that?

VALÈRE: Too bad her father died.

SGANARELLE: Oh. —And so you'll kindly cease
Your vain pursuit and leave the girl in peace.

VALÈRE: What! *My* pursuit?

SGANARELLE: Come, come, sir; don't deny it.
Drop this pretense; you're gaining nothing by it.

VALÈRE: Who said I loved her?

SGANARELLE: Someone whom I trust.

VALÈRE: But who? I ought to know.

SGANARELLE: Well, if you must,—
'Twas she herself.

VALÈRE: (Delighted) What! She? She knows!

SGANARELLE: 'Twas she who said it.
I trust, sir, you'll be good enough to credit
My word no less than hers. The girl's well-bred . . .

VALÈRE: I'm glad to hear that.

SGANARELLE: And not to be misled.

VALÈRE: Misled? By *me!*

SGANARELLE: She worships *me!*

VALÈRE: Ah, yes; undoubtedly. What else?

SGANARELLE: She charges me to tell you—

VALÈRE: Yes?

SGANARELLE: That she has understood
> What you have meant by trailing her about . . .
> She saw you ogling her.

VALÈRE: (*Triumphantly*) She saw me ogling her!

SGANARELLE: It banished any doubt
> She might have had. Your sighs are not melodious;
> In fact, she finds them. . . . (*Points to his nose*)

VALÈRE: Odious?

SGANARELLE: (Holding his nose) Odious!
> Yes, odious! Discard the notion
> That she has any wish for your devotion;
> She hopes you'll curb your zeal to make that known,
> Because her heart belongs to me alone.

VALÈRE: She sent you here, herself, to tell me this?

SGANARELLE: She did, *herself,* and begged me to dismiss
> All quibbling and to speak in downright fashion.
> She long has known of your obtrusive passion . . .

VALÈRE: (*Joyfully*) She knows of it!

SGANARELLE: But modesty restrained her
> From speaking of it sooner. It has pained her
> To see you dog her footsteps as a suitor. . . .

VALÈRE: But does she think . . .

SGANARELLE: Now cease to persecute her
> And look in some more possible direction.

VALÈRE: *She* tells me this?

SGANARELLE: She does. Her heart's affection
> Is mine, alone. In fact, I can't deny
> She says that I'm the apple of her eye!

VALÈRE: If this be true, of course I ought to quit the field,
> leaving her to you, . . . *if this be true!*

SGANARELLE: "if"! . . . You doubt me, then? Very well. You
> shall hear it from her own lips. Wait. (*He opens the
> door of his house*) Isabelle, Isabelle!

(Isabelle comes out)

ISABELLE: What! . . . That man! . . . You bring him here?
  And why?
  That he may plead his cause? You rate him high!
  Because *you* find his manners so disarming,
  You hope that *I* shall also find him charming?

SGANARELLE: Not so, my dear. Your heart is mine, I know,
  But this man simply will not have it so,
  And keeps the pet delusion in his head
  That I don't tell him what you really said .

ISABELLE: *(To Valère)* How can you doubt? Could words
  and looks reveal
  More clearly, still, the love and hate I feel?

VALÈRE: Dear Madam, what this gentleman advised me
  Was your own message, certainly surprised me;
  And still, before I draw the final curtain
  Across my fondest hope, I must be certain.
  Then, though your sentence be my sun's eclipse,
  I pray you, let me hear it from your lips!

ISABELLE: Then hear: He gave the message that I sent;
  You cannot doubt or question what I meant.
  I have a choice, if choice it can be named,
  Between two suitors; proud and unashamed
  I own that one I honor and adore
  With all my heart; . . . the other I abhor!
  The nearness of the one is my delight;
  The presence of the other is a blight;
  It is my dearest wish to be the wife
  Of one; but I would rather lose my life
  Than wed the other! Is my meaning clear?
  Oh, I have suffered long! If I am dear
  To him I love, let him no longer wait,
  But haste to blast the hopes of him I hate!

SGANARELLE: Yes, yes, my darling! He shall soon fulfill
  Your wishes.

ISABELLE: I shall count the hours until
  He makes me happy.

SGANARELLE: Happy you shall be!

ISABELLE: I know that I have been too bold and free, . . .

SGANARELLE: Oh, not at all!

ISABELLE: But would it not be hard
    To hide my soul from one whom I regard
    Already as my husband?

SGANARELLE: My poor dove!

ISABELLE: So let him quickly, quickly prove his love
    By doing what he should.

SGANARELLE: I understand.

ISABELLE: For only in our union may I find
    Contentment of the heart and peace of mind.

SGANARELLE: My precious one! My darling! Bless your fate!
    The day is near; you haven't long to wait.

VALÈRE: Yes, Isabelle. The part I have to play
    Is clear to me. I soon shall find a way
    To rid you of the one among those present
    Whose every act and word is so unpleasant.

ISABELLE: Do so! My hate for him is so intense,
    His very presence is a gross offense!

SGANARELLE: Now, now!

ISABELLE: So I offend by speaking so?
    Must I apologize?

SGANARELLE: Good gracious! No!
    And yet, I'm sorry. It must be distressing
    To learn that one is so unprepossessing.

ISABELLE: To speak less plainly, now, would be a crime.

VALÈRE: I understand.
    You haven't long to wait. In two days' time
    I shall so manage that your eyes shall rest
    No longer on this thing that you detest.
                    (Blackout)

ISABELLE: It's you! . . .
    I said, "Oh, heavens!" . . . you surprised me so.

SGANARELLE: Surprised you . . . doing what? Why are you
    here?

ISABELLE: A secret . . . and it's not my own to tell.

SGANARELLE: Now tell me.

ISABELLE: My sister; she . . . you saw her going out?

SGANARELLE: Yes, bound for that silly fete, as I recall.

ISABELLE: What *do* you think? She didn't go at all! (*Pointing to the house*) She's there!

SGANARELLE: Here! Why?

ISABELLE: She came to beg my aid . . .

SGANARELLE: Your aid for what?

ISABELLE: A plot.

SGANARELLE: A plot, the jade!

And you?

ISABELLE: I couldn't. It would be a sin.

Still she insisted, so I shut her in.

SGANARELLE: But *you* are *out;* . . . and why?

ISABELLE: What could I do

But hurry here in hope of meeting you!

And I'm so glad to find you. It's so nice

To have a good man's love and sound advice!

SGANARELLE: Now, now! . . . But why should Leonor come *here?*

ISABELLE: You know the world, and yet . . .

SGANARELLE: Go on, my dear.

ISABELLE: Can you believe those ears that hear me say

She loves the wretch whom we just sent away?

SGANARELLE: Valère?

ISABELLE: Valère. She loves him to distraction.

SGANARELLE: She does?

ISABELLE: She does; . . . God knows by what attraction.

Yes, they've been meeting for a year and more;

And when the thing began, the fellow swore

To marry her.

SGANARELLE: The dog! . . . Well, well, what then?

ISABELLE: Dressed up like me, she wants to meet

That rake below my window, in the street.

SGANARELLE: And then?

ISABELLE: She somehow hopes to reawake

His love for her.

SGANARELLE: What answer did you make?
    Not that you might?
ISABELLE: What? I! Now that's too bad!
    I said to her, "Oh, sister! Are you mad?
    How can you love so dissolute a rover?"
SGANARELLE: Yes, yes?
ISABELLE: "How can you dream of throwing over
    Your guardian, the man whom Heaven sent
    For you to marry as our father meant . . ."
SGANARELLE: Ariste!
ISABELLE: "He brought you up to be his wife;
    How can you wreck his hopes and spoil his life?"
SGANARELLE: Ariste! Ha, ha! Well, she is what he made her,
    And I'm not sorry.
ISABELLE: *(Eagerly)* But . . . you wouldn't aid her?
SGANARELLE: No-o. . . . Still, to play a trick upon my blind
    And doting brother, . . . that I wouldn't mind.
ISABELLE: Yes, yes!
SGANARELLE: No, no. . . . The business might reflect on you.
    So I'll just turn her out and lock the gate.
ISABELLE: Please don't do that; she's in a dreadful state
    And might make trouble. Leave her, please, to me.
SGANARELLE: All right.
ISABELLE: And hide yourself; don't let her see
    That you are watching; better let her go
    Without a word.
SGANARELLE: I promise. Just to show
    How much I love you, she shall go upon
    Her way, unscolded; but, when she is gone,
    I'll find my brother. With his well known views
    On freedom, he'll be charmed to hear this news.
ISABELLE: Oh, then you'll tell him?
SGANARELLE: Yes, beyond a doubt.
ISABELLE: Well . . . when you tell him, please leave my
      name out.
    I'll send her now. Good night, my dear. Don't fret.
SGANARELLE: All right, I won't. Until tomorrow, pet.

(Isabelle goes into the house, leaving the door open)

SGANARELLE: Aha! The wanton! How this news should tickle
  My dear old brother! What a pretty pickle
  He'll be in, after all his noble preachings,
  To see this fine result of his fine teachings!
  I'll rub his nose in this!
  (Isabelle appears U.L. in a cloak with a hood. As she pretends to talk to her sister, Sganarelle listens)

ISABELLE: No, no!

SGANARELLE: That's Isabelle.

ISABELLE: I wouldn't dare! I tell you no! It simply can't be done.
  It's wrong for *you,* and what a risk *I'd* run!
  That's all; that's final. Go at once. Good night.
  Run home, be good, and *do* keep out of sight!
  (She hides her face in the hood of her cloak and moves R.)

SGANARELLE: There goes the minx, . . . disguised, . . . the gadabout!
  She might come back; I'd better lock her out. *(He pantomimes locking the door)*

ISABELLE: He hasn't guessed. The twilight favors me.
  (She runs to Valère's and knocks at his door)

SGANARELLE: Valère's! Now we shall see what we shall see!

ISABELLE: I'm weak with fright. I'll knock again.
  (She knocks and Valère opens the door)

VALÈRE: Who's there?

ISABELLE: Hush! Hush! It's Isabelle. Valère, Valère!
  (They embrace)

SGANARELLE: *(Aside)* You lie, you minx! Have you no sense of shame?
  You take her clothes, her voice, her very name
  As if her honor were not worth a pin;
  And she so good, at home, and well locked in!

ISABELLE: But you must marry me, or even now . . .

VALÈRE: That is my dearest wish; it needs no vow
    To make it stronger. Be my guest until tomorrow,
       then my wife!
SGANARELLE: *Perhaps* she will! Yet . . . Ha, ha! Marry them
       to one another;
    Make two fools one! I'll get my doting brother
    To bless their union! Charming sentiment!
VALÈRE: I'll brave your tyrant; make him give consent
    To our espousal. But he shall not tear
    My treasure from me.

7

Scene from *The Cherry Orchard*

by Anton Chekhov
(1 man, 1 woman)

Near the end of the second act of the famous masterpiece by the great Russian playwright, the Andreyev family, owners of the cherry orchard, are in the orchard with some of their friends. In the afterglow following sunset a tramp comes by begging for money and unnerving several in the party, including Varya, the older foster daughter.

Now Anya, the gay and sunny younger daughter, seventeen, is alone with her friend, the earnest, idealistic student, Petya Trofimoff.

Although this is one of Chekhov's most lyrical scenes, it is not a typical love scene. Anya and Petya feel strongly toward each other, but Petya's passion is for the future of Russia which he envisions, and Anya is only in love with love.

The scene must be played with great honesty, even though Petya is somewhat carried away with his own rhetoric. A bare stage is all that is necessary.

The Cherry Orchard
by Anton Chekhov

ANYA: (*Laughing*) We should be grateful to that man. He frightened Varya and now we're by ourselves.

PETYA: Varya's afraid that we shall fall in love; so she never leaves us alone. Her narrow little mind can't comprehend that we're above love. To rise above petty unreal things which keep us from freedom and happiness—in that is the purpose of life, in that is its meaning. Onward! Undaunted, towards the brilliant star which shines far off! Onward! Let nothing hold you back, my friends.

ANYA: (*Clapping her hands*) You just speak wonderfully! (*Pause*) It's so glorious today!

PETYA: Yes, it's lovely weather.

ANYA: What have you done to me, Petya? Why don't I love the cherry orchard as I used? I loved it so much. I thought there was no better place on earth than our orchard.

PETYA: All Russia is our orchard. The world is wide and wonderful and full of beautiful places. (*Pause*) Think, Anya: your grandfather, your great-grandfather, and all your ancestors—they were slave owners. They owned living souls. Can't you see that from every cherry in this orchard, from every leaf, from the trunk of every tree, human creatures are looking at you? Can't you hear their voices? . . . to own living souls . . . it has done something to all of you, those who lived before and those who are living now. So that your mother and you, and your uncle, no longer realize that your lives are being lived at the expense of others, of the very people whom you don't let inside the door. . . . We are at least two hundred years behind the times. As yet we have nothing; no definite attitude to our past; we do nothing but philosophize;

we grumble and are discontented, or else we just drink vodka. But it's perfectly clear. Before we can begin to live in the present we must atone for our past; we must make a break with it. But such atonement can only be achieved by suffering, only by tremendous, unremitting effort. You must understand this, Anya.

ANYA: The house we live in doesn't belong to us any more. It hasn't been ours for ages. I'll leave it. I promise I will.

PETYA: Throw the keys into a deep well and go. Be free as the wind.

ANYA: *(Exalted)* Oh, you said that so wonderfully!

PETYA: Believe me, Anya, believe me! I'm not thirty yet. I'm young. I'm still a student, but I've been through a great deal. In the winter I am hungry, I am sick, I am anxious and as poor as a beggar. And wherever I go a cruel fate pursues me. Yet—always . . . at every minute, day or night, I feel a mysterious intimation, I feel an intimation of happiness, Anya. It's here . . .

ANYA: *(Dreamily)* The moon is rising.

(Yepihodov's guitar is heard. The moon rises. Varya is looking for Anya.)

VARYA: *(Offstage, calling)* Anya! Where are you?

PETYA: Yes, the moon is rising. *(Pause)* Here it is. Happiness. It's coming. Nearer and nearer. I can hear it. And if we can't see it, if we don't recognize it, what does it matter? Others will see it.

VARYA: *(Offstage)* Anya! Where are you?

PETYA: Varya *again!* . . . *(Angrily)* It's outrageous!

ANYA: Oh well. Let's go down to the river. It's nice there.

PETYA: Yes, let's go.

(They go)

VARYA: *(Offstage)* Anya! Anya!

8

Scene from *Love Your Neighbor*

A comedy by Albert Johnson
(2 men, 2 women)

When your neighbor is a dashing young bachelor who keeps bees, one of which has just stung you on the lip, and the bee man appears in person to administer his own home remedy for bee stings, interesting things can happen, especially when the man you are to marry tomorrow is suddenly very much in the way. That, in essence, is the situation, but there is more to the scene than the situation.

There is, for instance, the predicament in which Tessy, the vivacious coed with the sting, finds herself when indignation vies with amorous reaction to vibrations radiated by Johnny, the fast-working neighbor. There is also the bewilderment of Ozzy, the fiancé, and the coyness of kid sister Dora to be enacted.

Although stairs are called for in the setting, the scene may be played on a bare stage.

Love Your Neighbor
by Albert Johnson

JOHNNY: (*Enters from hall with a box of candy*) Good afternoon.

DORA: Hello, Johnny.

JOHNNY: (*Stopping to empty his pipe in the fireplace*) I hear my bees have been trespassing on private property.

TESSY: They certainly have.

JOHNNY: Forgive them their trespasses as— (*He notices Tessy, and something clicks between them.*) Oh, hello.

TESSY: Hello.

JOHNNY: I'm Johnny.

TESSY: I'm Tessy.

JOHNNY: (*Crossing to Tessy and handing her the box of candy*) Sorry about my bee. I thought I'd come over and see if I could administer first aid. I'm pretty good with bee stings.

TESSY: (*Putting the box of candy on the table D.C.*) I imagine you've had lots of experience.

JOHNNY: (*Crossing D.R.*) Well, I have had some experience with bees.

OZZY: (*Rising; in disgust*) Well, I haven't, and if you don't mind—

TESSY: Ozzy, run upstairs to the bath and get me some ointment or something. This soda isn't much good.

OZZY: Tessy, for Pete's sake—

TESSY: That's a good boy, Ozzy. Please. My lip is killing me. Dora will show you where to look.

DORA: Delighted. This way, Ozzy—

OZZY: But, but, Tessy—

DORA: (*Crossing and pulling Ozzy upstairs*) Come on, Ozzy, I want to show you my hope chest, anyway.

TESSY: I think you'll find something in the medicine cabinet.

DORA: Sure. It may take us quite a while, but we'll find something. Won't we, Ozzy?

OZZY: (*With another look toward Tessy*) Well . . . well . . . well, okay.

(*He and Dora go upstairs. Tessy crosses D.R.*)

JOHNNY: Yes, you might say I know bees from stem to stern. Do you mind if I have a look at that sting?

(*He takes Tessy's chin in his hand and gazes at her lips. Their eyes dance at each other.*)

JOHNNY: (*Still gazing*) Not bad, not bad.

TESSY: What do you mean, not bad? That bee gave me everything he had.

JOHNNY: She, not he. It's the female of the species that causes all the mischief.

TESSY: It's the female that produces the honey, too, isn't it?

JOHNNY: (*Grinning at her*) You said it.

(*He has taken his hand from her chin now, but they still glance at each other with interest*)

TESSY: It was silly of me to rush to the telephone like that, but I was pretty mad.

JOHNNY: Mad? I havn't heard language that rugged since I left the Marines.

TESSY: After all, how would you feel if a vagrant bee came into your house uninvited and sat down on your lip?

JOHNNY: If I were a bee, don't think I'd pass up lips like those. (*Having another close look at her lip*) First thing you want to do is get the stinger out.

(*He seats Tessy on settee, while he stands L. of it. He again takes Tessy's chin in his hand.*) Steady now. (*He starts removing the stinger from her lip*) Know what happens when a bee loses her stinger?

TESSY: It dies. Thank goodness that's one less.

JOHNNY: That only leaves about 299 thousand, nine hundred and ninety-nine—in that hive. Of course, I've got a lot of other hives. I've got hives, and hives, and hives.

TESSY: I don't care if you've got chiggers, your bees shouldn't be so promiscuous.

JOHNNY: (*Removing the stinger*) There, no more stinger. How does it feel now?

TESSY: Terrible.

JOHNNY: You know, when I was a kid, my mother had a perfect remedy for bee stings.

TESSY: What was it?

JOHNNY: I'll show you. (*He kisses her gently but enthusiastically on the lips*)

TESSY: (*Obviously not displeased, rises quickly*) No wonder your bees are promiscuous. They get it from you.

JOHNNY: But you will admit my bees have discriminating taste.

TESSY: I don't know. I didn't taste it.

JOHNNY: (*Starting to kiss her again*) Well, maybe we'd better do a retake.

TESSY: (*This time evading him*) No. No. I didn't mean that. I meant the bee.

JOHNNY: You're going to love my bees when you get to know them better.

TESSY: (*Looking in mantel mirror*) I'd have to love them a lot to go around kissing their little stingers.

JOHNNY: You ought to be glad to have them around. Think of all the pollen they spread.

TESSY: Well, they don't have to spread it on me.

JOHNNY: I would if I were a bee.

TESSY: Are you sure you aren't one? You certainly peddle a mean line of honey.

JOHNNY: I don't ordinarily. Usually I'm shy as a sheep; but when I saw you . . . well . . . I was like the bee, I found you irresistible.

TESSY: Does that mean I'm going to have you buzzing around as well as your bees?

JOHNNY: Are you glad?

TESSY: *(Crossing to C.)* Would you like me to be glad?

JOHNNY: *(Sitting on settee)* Well, you ought to be. At least you ought to be grateful—for the bees, I mean.

TESSY: Oh?

JOHNNY: Why, you wouldn't have any flowers or any fruit or even any squash if my bees didn't come over and get the little boy blossoms acquainted with the little girl blossoms. See what I mean?

TESSY: If they're going to spend all their time over here, I ought to charge you grazing fee.

JOHNNY: *(Rising and coming toward her)* On the contrary, I ought to collect for all the pollinating they do.

TESSY: *(Sitting on table)* What's an ex-Marine doing running an apiary anyway?

JOHNNY: *(Standing near Tessy, he picks up candy and offers it to her. Tessy takes a piece)* Oh, the bees are just a beginning. Haven't you heard about my candy? It's running other candies right off the market. And I'm going to put up a wax factory. Look, I'd like to have you come over and see my place and meet my bees.

TESSY: Thank you, I've already met them. *(She crosses to piano)*

JOHNNY: *(Following her)* Did you ever see bees at work? Fascinating. Do you know that a queen bee thinks nothing at all of having two or three thousand baby bees at once? Think of that many tiny feet pitter-pattering around.

TESSY: That's a lot of pitter-pattering. *(She does a trill on piano)*

JOHNNY: Yeah, but I like the idea, don't you?

TESSY: Well, I've heard about such things. In college I took a course in marriage.

JOHNNY: Oh, that's swell. That's perfect. I'd like us to have lots and lots of bees, and lots of horses and dogs, and lots of children. Oh, not right away, of course. Come on over and meet my horses and my dogs and my mother. (*He slips his arm around her*)

TESSY: I've met your mother. She's very nice. (*Crossing toward C., she takes another piece of candy*)

JOHNNY: You bet; but you ought to meet my dogs. I've got two of the swellest setters.

TESSY: (*Enthusiastically*) Irish setters? I love them. (*Tessy comes back toward Johnny*)

JOHNNY: Well, one's Irish. The other, I don't know. I think she may be part Scotch . . . Gee, I feel good! I haven't felt so good—You know, a fella goes along dreaming about something like this, then he gets to wondering if it will ever happen. Then all of a sudden he meets the right girl and—Well, you begin to get ideas.

TESSY: (*Crossing toward stairs*) You certainly do. I think I'd better tell you—

JOHNNY: All because one of my bees came over for a little reconnoitering.

TESSY: Listen, Johnny Jones. I don't know how to tell you, but—

JOHNNY: Hold it. I just thought of something. That bee—the one that stung you—Think how indebted we are to that lttle bee. She gave up her life to bring us together.

TESSY: Very touching. (*She feels her lip*) Especially touching the way it made its sacrifice.

JOHNNY: (*Coming toward her*) By the way, how's the sting?

TESSY: (*Standing on bottom step*) Terrible. Everything's terrible. Johnny, I'm—

JOHNNY: Then it's time it had another treatment. (*He kisses her again, as Dora comes down the stairs, followed by Ozzy*)

DORA: (*Waving a tube of something*) All we could find was toothpaste.

ozzy: (*Discovering the kissing couple*) Hey! What's coming off here?

JOHNNY: Who is this chap?

TESSY: I've been trying to tell you. This is Ozzy Fredrick—

JOHNNY: (*Starting to take Tessy in his arms again*) We'll ignore him.

TESSY: He's my fiancé!

JOHNNY: Your what?

TESSY: I'm to be married tomorrow. (*She puts her hand to her lip and is practically in tears*) Oh, dear, my lip! (*She sinks upon stairs*)

Permission to reprint granted by Walter H. Baker Company, Boston; © 1945 Row, Peterson & Co.

9

The Man Who
Married a Dumb Wife

by Anatole France
A condensation
(4 men, 2 women)

This is a cutting of a very popular play by a playwright who had a great flair for high comedy. Since it is a cutting rather than a single scene, it is self-explanatory except for pointing out that the comedy must be played to the hilt.

The charm of the play is in its delectable nonsense. The trick is to make the impossible seem entirely probable.

No special setting is necessary. A few chairs and a table or two may be arranged to suit the blocking. It is a fun play, but the characters must take themselves seriously.

The Man Who Married a Dumb Wife
by Anatole France

Scene: The home of Leonard Botal.
(Leonard Botal comes down the stairs)

MASTER ADAM: *(Entering)* Good day, Master Leonard, I am delighted to see you again.

LEONARD: Good morning, Master Adam, how have you been this long time that I haven't set eyes on you?

MASTER ADAM: Well, very well. And I hope I find you the same, your Honour.

LEONARD: Fairly so, fairly so.

MASTER ADAM: Only fairly so? Perhaps you are lonely. Why don't you get married?

LEONARD: What, what! Don't you know, Master Adam, that I *have* just been married? *(They sit down on the bench in front of the table)* Yes, only last month, to a girl from one of our best country families, young and handsome, Catherine Momichel. But alas! she is dumb. Now you know my affliction.

MASTER ADAM: Your wife is dumb?

LEONARD: Alas, yes.

MASTER ADAM: Quite, quite dumb?

LEONARD: As a fish.

MASTER ADAM: And you didn't notice it till after you'd married her?

LEONARD: Oh, I couldn't help noticing it, of course, but it didn't seem to make so much difference to me then as it does now. I considered her beauty, and her property and thought of nothing but the advantages of the match and the happiness I should have with her. But now these matters seem less important, and I do wish she could talk; that would be a real intellectual pleasure for me, and, what's more, a practical advantage for the household. What does a Judge need most in his house? Why, a good-looking wife, to receive the suitors pleasantly, and, by subtle suggestions, gently bring them to the point of making proper presents, so that their cases may receive—more careful attention. You see, Master Adam, what I lose by having a dumb wife. I'm not worth half as much. . . . And the worst of it is, I'm losing my spirits, and almost my wits, with it all.

MASTER ADAM: There's no reason in that, now, your Honour. Just consider the thing closely, and you will find some advantages in your case as it stands, and no mean ones neither.

LEONARD: No, no, Master Adam; you don't understand. Think!—When I hold my wife in my arms—a woman as beautiful as the finest carved statue, at least so I think—and quite as silent, that I'm sure of—it makes me feel queer and uncanny.

MASTER ADAM: What notions!

LEONARD: Worse yet! What with having a dumb wife, I'm going dumb myself. Sometimes I catch myself using signs, as she does. The other day, on the Bench, I even pronounced judgment in pantomime, and condemned a man to the gallows, just by dumb show and gesticulation.

MASTER ADAM: Enough! Say no more!

LEONARD: Now you know the reason why I'm in low spirits.

MASTER ADAM: I won't contradict you; I admit that your reason is full and sufficient. But perhaps there's a remedy. Tell me: Is your wife deaf as well as dumb?

LEONARD: Catherine is no more deaf that you and I are; even less, I might say. She can hear the very grass growing.

MASTER ADAM: Then the case is not hopeless. 'Tis but child's play for a doctor to untie their tongues. The operation is so simple that it's done every day to puppies that can't learn to bark. Must a countryman like me come to town to tell you that there's a famous doctor, just around the corner from your own house, Master Simon, who has made a reputation for loosing the tongues of the ladies of Paris?

LEONARD: Is this true, Master Adam? Aren't you deceiving me? Aren't you speaking as a lawyer in court?

MASTER ADAM: I'm speaking as a friend, and telling you the plain truth.

LEONARD: Then I'll send for this famous doctor—and that right away.

MASTER ADAM: As you please. . . . But before you call him in, you must reflect soberly, and consider what it's really best to do. For, take it all in all, though there are some disadvantages in having a dumb wife, there are some advantages, too. . . . Well, good day, your Honour, my dear old school-fellow. (*They go together to the street door. They bow low to each other. Exit Master Adam*)

LEONARD: (*At the door, calling*) Alison! Alison! The wench never hears me; she is in the kitchen, as usual, up-setting the soup and the servants. She's a lazy little goose.

ALISON: (*Entering*) Present, your Honour.

LEONARD: Go straight to the famous doctor, Master Simon, who lives at the Sign of the Dragon, and tell him to come to my house at once, to treat a dumb woman. . . .

ALISON: Yes, your Honour. (*Alison starts off, running, to the right*)

LEONARD: Go the nearest way, not round by the New Bridge, to watch the jugglers. I know you, you slow-poke; there's not such another cheat and loafer in ten counties.

(*Alison comes back, slowly, across stage, and stops*)

ALISON: Sir, you wrong me. . . .

LEONARD: Be off! and bring the famous doctor back with you.

ALISON: (*Bolting off to the left*) Yes, your Honour.

LEONARD: (*Going up and sitting down at the table, which is loaded with briefbags*) I have fourteen verdicts to render today. And that is no small labor, because a decree, to do credit to the Judge, must be cleverly worded, subtle, elegant, and adorned with all the

ornaments both of style and of thought. The ideas
must be pleasingly conceived and playfully expressed.
Where should one show one's wit, if not in a verdict?
*(Catherine enters from the upper stairway door; she
curtsies to the audience and then sits on the window-
seat, embroidering. Leonard looks up from his work
at the table, and seeing Catherine, goes to her and
kisses her as she rises to meet him. She makes a curtsy,
kisses him in return, and listens with pleased attention)*
Good morning, my love. . . . I didn't even hear you
come down. You are like the fairy forms in the stories,
that seem to glide upon air, or like the dreams which
the gods, as poets tell, send down to happy mortals.
(Catherine shows her pleasure in his compliments)
My love, you are a marvel of nature, and a triumph
of art; you have all charms but speech. *(Catherine
turns away, sobbing slightly)* Shouldn't you be glad
to have that, too? *(She turns back intensely interested)* Shouldn't you be pleased to show your wit?
(She waves her handkerchief in glee) Shouldn't you
like to tell your husband how you love him? Wouldn't
it be delightful to call him your treasure and sweet-
heart? Yes, surely! . . . *(They rise. Catherine is full
of pleased animation)* Well, I've a piece of good news
for you, my love. . . . A great doctor is coming here
presently, who can make you talk. . . . *(Catherine
shows her satisfaction, dancing gracefully up and
down)* He will untie your tongue and never hurt you
a bit. Now go back to your room, my dear, and I will
bring the doctor to you when he comes. *(Catherine
smiles and exits)*
(Enter Alison, then Master Simon and Master Jean)
ALISON: Your Honour, here's the great doctor you sent for.
MASTER SIMON: *(Bowing)* Yes, I am Master Simon him-

self. . . . And this is Master Jean, surgeon. You called for our services?

LEONARD: Yes, sir, to make a dumb woman speak.

MASTER SIMON: Say, rather, I shall order the operation. I command, Master Jean executes. . . . Have you your instruments with you, Master Jean?

MASTER JEAN: Yes, Master. (*He unfolds the large cloth case of instruments and holds it up, disclosing a huge saw with two-inch teeth, and knives, pincers, scissors, a skewer, a bit-stock, an enormous bit, etc.*)

LEONARD: I hope, sirs, you don't intend to use all those?

MASTER SIMON: One must never be caught unarmed by a patient.

MASTER SIMON: Now we are here, shall we go see the patient?

LEONARD: I will show you the way, gentlemen.

MASTER SIMON: After you, Master Jean, you go first.

MASTER JEAN: I'll go first, since the place of honor is the rear.

(*They follow Leonard off. The curtains close to indicate a lapse of four or five hours*)

(*The curtain opens. Leonard is discovered*)

MASTER ADAM: (*Entering*) Good afternoon, your Honour. How are you this afternoon?

LEONARD: I've been entertaining the flower of the medical faculty here. (*Suddenly seizing him by the shoulders and shaking him*) 'Twas your advice brought this trouble upon me.

MASTER ADAM: Why, what do you mean?

LEONARD: I sent for the famous doctor you told me about, Master Simon. He came, with a surgeon; he examined my wife, Catherine, from head to foot, to see if she was dumb. Then, the surgeon cut my dear Catherine's tongue-ligament, and she spoke.

MASTER ADAM: She spoke? And what did she say?

LEONARD: She said: "Bring me my looking-glass!" And, seeing me quite overcome by my feelings, she added, "You old goose, you shall give me a new satin gown and a velvet-trimmed cape for my birthday."

MASTER ADAM: And she kept on talking?

LEONARD: She hasn't stopped yet.

MASTER ADAM: And yet you don't thank me for my advice; you don't thank me for having sent you to that wonderful doctor? Aren't you overjoyed to hear your wife speak?

LEONARD: (*Softly*) Yes, certainly. I thank you with all my heart, Master Adam, and I am overjoyed to hear my wife speak.

MASTER ADAM: No! You do not show as much satisfaction as you ought to. There is something you are keeping back—something that's worrying you.

LEONARD: Where did you get such a notion?

MASTER ADAM: From your face. . . . What is bothering you? Isn't your wife's speech clear?

LEONARD: Yes, it's clear—and abundant. I must admit, its abundance would be a trial to me if it kept up at the rate which it started at.

MASTER ADAM: Ah! . . . I feared *that* beforehand, your Honour. But you mustn't be cast down too soon. Perhaps this flood of words will ebb. It is the first overflow of a spring too long bottled up. . . . My best congratulations, your Honour. (*Exit Master Adam*)

(*Catherine is heard off stage singing. Leonard starts, shakes his head, hurries to his writing-table, and sits down to work. Catherine, still singing, enters gaily, and goes to him at the table*)

LEONARD: (*Reading*) "Statement, on behalf of Ermeline-Jacinthe-Marthe de la Garandiere, gentlewoman."

CATHERINE: (*Standing behind his chair, and first finishing her song: "La dee ra, dee ra, day," then speaking with great volubility*) What are you doing, my dear? You seem busy. You work too much. (*She goes to the window-seat and takes up her embroidery*) Aren't you afraid it will make you ill? You must rest once in a while. Why don't you tell me what you are doing, dear?

LEONARD: My love, I . . .

CATHERINE: Is it such a great secret? Can't I know about it?

LEONARD: My love, I . . .

CATHERINE: If it's a secret, don't tell me.

LEONARD: Won't you give me a chance to answer? I am examining a case and preparing to draw up a verdict on it.

CATHERINE: Is drawing up a verdict so very important?

LEONARD: Most certainly it is. (*Catherine sits at the window singing and humming to herself, and looking out*) In the first place, people's honour, their liberty, and sometimes even their life, may depend on it; and furthermore, the Judge must show therein both the depth of his thought and the finish of his style.

CATHERINE: Then examine your case and prepare your verdict, my dear. I'll be silent.

LEONARD: That's right. . . . "Ermeline-Jacinthe-Marthe de la Garandiere, gentlewoman . . ."

CATHERINE: My dear, which do you think would be more becoming to me, a damask gown, or a velvet suit with a Turkish skirt?

LEONARD: I don't know, I . . .

CATHERINE: I think a flowered satin would suit my age best, especially a light-colored one, with a *small* flower pattern.

LEONARD: Perhaps so. But . . .

CATHERINE: And don't you think, my dear, that it is quite improper to have a hoop-skirt very full? Of course, a skirt must have *some* fullness . . . or else you don't seem dressed at all; so, we mustn't let it be scanty. But, my dear, you wouldn't want me to have room enough to hide a pair of lovers under my hoops, now would you? That fashion won't last, I'm sure; some day the court ladies will give it up, and then every woman in town will make haste to follow their example. Don't you think so?

LEONARD: Yes; Yes! But . . .

CATHERINE: Now, about high heels. . . . They must be made just right. A woman is judged by her footgear—you can always tell a real fine lady by her shoes. You agree with me, don't you, dear?

LEONARD: Yes, yes, *yes*, but . . .

CATHERINE: Then write out your verdict. I shan't say another word.

LEONARD: That's right.

(*Reading and making notes*) "Now, the guardian of the said young lady, namely Hugo Thomas of Piedeloup, gentleman, stole from the said young lady her——"

CATHERINE: My dear, if one were to believe the wife of the Chief Justice, the world has grown very corrupt; it is going to the bad; young men nowadays don't marry; they prefer to hang about rich old ladies and meanwhile the poor girls are left to wither on their maiden stalks. Do you think it's as bad as all that? Do answer me, dear.

LEONARD: My darling, won't you please be silent one moment? Or go and talk somewhere else? I'm all at sea.

CATHERINE: There, there, dear; don't worry. I shan't say another word! Not a word!

LEONARD: Good. (*Writing*) "The said Piedeloup, gentleman, counting both hay crops and apple crops . . ."

CATHERINE: My dear, we shall have for supper tonight some minced mutton and what's left of that goose one of your suitors gave us. Tell me, is that enough? Shall you be satisfied with it? I hate being mean, and like to set a good table, but what's the use of serving courses which will only be sent back to the pantry untouched? The cost of living is getting higher all the time. Chickens, and salads, and meats, and fruit have all gone up so, it will soon be cheaper to order dinner sent in by a caterer.

LEONARD: I beg you . . . (*Writing*) "An orphan by birth . . ."

CATHERINE: Yes, that's what we're coming to. No home life any more. You'll see. Why, a capon, or a partridge, or a hare, cost less all stuffed and roasted than if you buy them alive at the market. That is because the cook-shops buy in large quantities and get a big discount; so they can sell to us at a profit. I don't say we ought to get our regular meals from the cook-shop. We can do our everyday plain cooking at home, and it's better to; but when we invite people in, or give a formal dinner party, then it saves time and money to have the dinner sent in. Why, at less than an hour's notice, the cook-shops and cake-shops will get up a dinner for a dozen, or twenty, or fifty people; the cook-shop will send in meat and poultry, the caterer will send galantines and sauces and relishes, the pastry-cook will send pies and tarts and sweets and desserts; and it's all so convenient. Now, don't you think so yourself, Leonard?

LEONARD: Please, please! (*Leonard tries to write through the following speech, murmuring*) "An orphan by birth, a capon by birth," etc.

CATHERINE: It's no wonder everything goes up. People are getting more extravagant every day. If they are entertaining a friend, or even a relative, they don't think they can do with only three courses, soup, meat, and dessert. No, they have to have meats in five or six different styles, with so many sauces, or dressings, or pasties. Now, don't you think that is going too far, my dear? For my part I just cannot understand how people can take pleasure in stuffing themselves with so many kinds of food. Not that I despise a good table; why, I'm even a bit of an epicure myself. "Not too plenty, but dainty," suits my taste. Now, what I like best of all is . . .

LEONARD: (*His head in his hands*) I shall go mad! I know I shall go mad.

CATHERINE: (*Running to the table behind him*) My dear, I just shan't say another word—not a single word. For I can see that my chattering *might* possibly disturb your work.

LEONARD: If you would only do as you say!

CATHERINE: (*Returning to her place*) I shan't even open my lips.

LEONARD: Splendid!

CATHERINE: (*Busily embroidering*) You see, dear, I'm not saying another word.

LEONARD: Yes.

CATHERINE: I'm letting you work in perfect peace and quiet.

LEONARD: Yes.

CATHERINE: And write out your verdict quite undisturbed. Is it almost done?

LEONARD: It never will be—if you don't keep still. (*Writing*) "Item, One hundred twenty pounds a year, which the said unworthy guardian stole from the poor orphan girl . . ."

CATHERINE: Listen! Ssh-sh! Listen! Didn't you hear a cry of fire? (*Leonard runs to the window, looks out, and then shakes his head at Catherine*) I thought I did. But perhaps I may have been mistaken. Is there anything so terrifying as a fire? Fire is even worse than water. Last year I saw the houses on Exchange Bridge burn up. What confusion! What havoc! The people threw their furniture into the river, and jumped out of the windows. They didn't know what they were about; you see, fear drove them out of their senses.

LEONARD: Lord, have mercy upon me!

CATHERINE: Oh! What makes you groan so, dear? *Tell* me, tell me what is the matter?

LEONARD: I can't endure it another minute.

CATHERINE: You must rest, Leonard. You mustn't work so hard. It isn't reasonable. You have no right to . . .

LEONARD: Will you never be still?

CATHERINE: Now, don't be cross, dear. I'm not saying another word.

LEONARD: I've got to the point where I can't answer for the consequences; I feel capable of committing any crime. (*Calling*) Alison! Alison! The wench! Alison! (*Enter Alison*) Go quick and find the famous Doctor, Master Simon, and tell him to come back here at once for a matter far more needful and urgent than before.

ALISON: Yes, your Honour. (*Exit*)

CATHERINE: What's the matter, my dear? You seem excited. Perhaps the air is close. No? It's the east wind, then, don't you think?—or the fish you ate for dinner?

LEONARD: (*Frantically*) Oh, how I regret, you saucy baggage, that I had your tongue loosed. Don't you worry, though—the famous doctor shall soon make you more dumb than ever you were.

(*He catches up armfuls of the briefbags which are piled on his cupboard of refuge, and throws them at Catherine's head; she jumps and runs off in terror, crying*)

CATHERINE: Help! Murder! My husband's gone mad! Help! help!

(*Master Jean and Master Simon enter*)

MASTER JEAN: Your Honour, I bid you good day. Here is Master Simon.

LEONARD: Master Simon, I was in haste to see you. I urgently beg for your services.

MASTER SIMON: For yourself? What is your disease? Where is the pain?

LEONARD: No! For my wife; the one who was dumb.

MASTER SIMON: Has she any trouble now?

LEONARD: None at all. I have all the trouble now.

MASTER SIMON: What? The trouble is with you, and it's your wife you want cured?

LEONARD: Master Simon, she talks too much. You should have given her speech, but not so much speech. Since you've cured her of her dumbness, she drives me mad. I cannot bear another word from her. I've called you in to make her dumb again.

MASTER SIMON: 'Tis impossible!

LEONARD: What's that? You can't take away the power of speech which you gave her?

MASTER SIMON: No! That I cannot do. My skill is great, but it stops short of that.

(*Leonard in despair turns to each of them in succession*)

MASTER JEAN: We cannot do it.

LEONARD: Can this be true?

MASTER SIMON: Sir, you dare not so offend me as to doubt it.

LEONARD: Then I am a ruined man. There's nothing left for me to do but tie a stone around my neck and jump into the Seine. (*He rushes to the window and tries to jump out, but is held back by the doctors*) I cannot live in this hubbub. (*The doctors drag him back*) If you don't want me to drown myself straightway, then you doctors must find me some cure.

MASTER SIMON: There is none, I tell you, for your wife. But there might be one for you, if you would consent to take it.

LEONARD: You give me a little hope. Explain it, for heaven's sake.

MASTER SIMON: For the clack of a wife, there's but one cure in life. Let her husband be deaf. 'Tis the only relief.

LEONARD: What do you mean?

MASTER SIMON: Just what I say.

LEONARD: Make me really deaf? Oh! . . . (*He starts to rise, but is pushed back by Master Simon, who stands directly in front of him*)

MASTER SIMON: Do you see any disadvantages in becoming deaf?

LEONARD: Certainly I do!

MASTER JEAN: You think so?

MASTER SIMON: You are a Judge. What disadvantage is there in a Judge's being deaf? What harm could come to justice thereby?

MASTER JEAN: No harm at all. Quite the contrary. Master Leonard could then hear neither lawyers nor prosecutors, and so would run no risk of being deceived by a lot of lies.

LEONARD: That's true.

SIMON: He will judge all the better.

LEONARD: Maybe so. But how do you perform this . . .

MASTER JEAN: This cure.

MASTER SIMON: By means of a certain white powder which I have in my medicine-case; a pinch of it, placed in the ear, is enough to make you as deaf as heaven when it's angry, or as deaf as a post.

LEONARD: Many thanks, Master Simon, keep your powder. I will not be made deaf.

CATHERINE: (*Enters singing*) What a fine large assembly! I am your humble servant, gentlemen. (*She curtsies*)

MASTER SIMON: Well, madam? Aren't you pleased with us? Didn't we do our work well in loosing your tongue?

CATHERINE: Fairly well, sirs; and I'm truly grateful to you. At first, to be sure, I could speak but haltingly, and bring out only a few words; now, however, I have some degree of facility, but I use it with great moderation, for a garrulous wife is a scourge in the house. Yes, gentlemen, I should be in despair if you could so much as suspect me of loquacity, or if you could

think for a moment that any undue desire to talk
could get hold of me. And so, I beg you to let me
justify myself here and now in the eyes of my husband, who, for some inconceivable reason, has become prejudiced against me, and taken it into his
head that my conversation bothered him while he was
drawing up a decree. . . . Yes, a decree in favour of
an orphan girl deprived of her father and mother in
the flower of her youth. But no matter for that. I was
sitting beside him and hardly saying a single word
to him. My only speech was my presence. Can a husband object to that? Can he take it ill when his wife
stays with him and seeks to enjoy his company, as
she ought?

(*She goes to her husband and sits down beside him.
During the rest of the speech all those present, one
after another, sink down in exhaustion at listening
to her*)

The more I think of it, the less I can understand your
impatience. What can have caused it? You must stop
pretending it was my talkativeness. That idea won't
hold water one moment. My dear, you must have some
grievance against me which I know nothing about; I
beg you to tell me what it is. You *owe* me an explanation, and as soon as I find out what displeased you I
will see to it that you have no reason to complain of
the same thing again—if only you'll tell me what it is.
For I am eager to save you from the slightest reason
for dissatisfaction. My mother used to say: "Between
husband and wife, there should be no secrets." And
she was quite right. Married people have only too
often brought down terrible catastrophes on themselves or their households just because they didn't tell
each other everything. My dear, you can speak freely
before these gentlemen. I know I have done nothing

wrong, so whatever you say can only prove the more clearly how innocent I am.

LEONARD: (*Who has for some time been trying in vain by gestures and exclamations to stop Catherine's flow of words, and has been showing signs of extreme impatience*) The powder! Give me the powder! Master Simon, your powder—your white powder, for God's sake!

MASTER SIMON: Never was a deafness-producing powder more needed, that's sure. Be so kind as to sit down, your Honour. Master Jean will inject the powder in your ears.

(*The doctors crowd about Leonard, and inject the powder first in one ear and then in the other*)

MASTER JEAN: Gladly, sir, gladly.

MASTER SIMON: There! 'Tis done.

CATHERINE: (*To the doctor*) Make my husband hear reason. Tell him that he must listen to me, that it's unheard of to condemn a wife without letting her state her case, tell him it's not right to throw briefbags at your wife's head—yes, he threw briefbags at my head —unless you are forced to it by some very strong feeling or reason. . . . Or no!—I'll tell him myself. (*To Leonard*) My dear, answer me, have I ever failed you in anything? Am I a naughty woman? Am I a bad wife? No, I have been faithful to my duty, I may even say I have loved my duty . . .

I have loved my duty . . .

LEONARD: (*His face expressing beatitude, as he calmly twirls his thumbs*) 'Tis delicious. I can't hear a thing!

10

Suggested Additional Plays

(Scenes for 1 man, 1 woman)

Ah, Wilderness (Eugene O'Neill)
Angel Street (Patrick Hamilton)
The Barretts of Wimpole Street (Rudolf Besier)
The Bluebird (Maurice Maeterlinck)
Candida (George Bernard Shaw)
The Dark at the Top of the Stairs (William Inge)
Dear Brutus (J. M. Barrie)
The Glass Menagerie (Tennessee Williams)
Hay Fever (Noel Coward)
Major Barbara (George Bernard Shaw)
A Majority of One (Leonard Spigelgass)
Our Town (Thornton Wilder)
Pygmalion (George Bernard Shaw)
The Red Peppers (Noel Coward)
St. Joan (George Bernard Shaw)
Summer and Smoke (Tennessee Williams)
Tovarich (Jacques Deval)
Winterset (Maxwell Anderson)

(Scenes for 2 women)

Anastasia (Guy Bolton)

Antigone (Jean Anouilh)
Arsenic and Old Lace (Joseph Kesselring)
The Cave Dwellers (William Saroyan)
The Desk Set (William Marchant)
I Remember Mama (John van Druten)
Ladies in Waiting (Cyril Campion)
Liliom (Ferenc Molnar)
A Majority of One (Leonard Spigelgass)
Mary of Scotland (Maxwell Anderson)
The Miracle Worker (William Gibson)
Summer and Smoke (Tennessee Williams)
Our Town (Thornton Wilder)

(Scenes for 2 men)

I Remember Mama (John van Druten)
Our Town (Thornton Wilder)
Romanoff and Juliet (Peter Ustinov)

(Scenes for 1 man, 2 women)

Arsenic and Old Lace (Joseph Kesselring)
The Cave Dwellers (William Saroyan)
Cyrano de Bergerac (Edmond Rostand)
Hay Fever (Noel Coward)
A Majority of One (Leonard Spigelgass)

(Scenes for 2 men, 1 woman)

The Bald Soprano (Eugene Ionesco)
Cyrano de Bergerac (Edmond Rostand)
The Fantasticks (Tom Jones and Harvey Schmidt)
Inherit the Wind (Jerome Lawrence and Robert E. Lee)
Our Town (Thornton Wilder)
St. Joan (George Bernard Shaw)

(Scenes for 2 men, 2 women)

Dear Me, The Sky is Falling (Leonard Spigelgass)
The Importance of Being Earnest (Oscar Wilde)
A Majority of One (Leonard Spigelgass)
Mary, Mary (Jean Kerr)

(Scenes for 3 women)

The Diary of Anne Frank (Frances Goodrich and Albert
    Hackett)
The Madwoman of Chaillot (Jean Girardoux)
Our Town (Thornton Wilder)